School-Age Ideas & Activities for After-School Programs

2nd Edition, Revised

by

Karen Haas-Foletta
Michele Cogley
Lori Ottolini Geno

Photos by Craig Burleigh
Illustrations by Mary R. Thomason

School-Age NOTES ● Nashville TN

PUBLISHER'S NOTES:

Words have been used in this text that the authors have reason to believe constitute trade names. However, neither the presence nor absence of a trademark designation should be regarded as affecting the legal status of any trademark.

Throughout this text you will see references to both "after-school programs" and "school-age care" or "SAC." These references are interchangeable and mean the same thing: programs that care for children between the ages of five and 14 before and after school, during holidays and the summer.

ISBN: 0-917505-20-4

10 9 8 7 6 5 4 3 2 1

Published by School-Age NOTES, P.O. Box 40205, Nashville TN 37204-0205

Dedications & Acknowledgements

Dedicated to:

Jon Foletta, Karen's husband

Kevin Geno, Lori's husband

Our Children:

    Nicholas Foletta and Kyle Foletta

    Chris Bigler Pengelley, Azrael Bigler, Matthew and Nathaniel Cogley

    Gregory Geno and Christopher Geno

And Michele's grandchildren, Jessica and Brandon

We dedicate this book in memory of
Richard T. Scofield
who shall remain an inspiration, mentor, and visionary to all
who are working to make the lives
of children, youth, and their families better.

Acknowledgements:

We would like to thank Karen's mother, Carolyn Buhai Haas, co-author of *I Saw a Purple Cow, A Pumpkin in a Pear Tree, Children are Children are Children, Backyard Vacation, Purple Cow to the Rescue!*, and the author of *The Big Book of Fun* and *Look at Me.* She assisted with ideas and editing the first edition of the book.

We would like to thank the Parent Board of Directors, staff and children of West Portal C.A.R.E, Inc. and Cipriani After-School Care, Inc. This is where our ideas and activities are tested and proven successful. We are also grateful to Linda Tanimasa for her assistance with the indoor/outdoor games section.

Michele would like to thank all the wonderful educators who have shared their expertise and creativity with her over the years.

About the Authors

Karen Haas-Foletta is the Executive Director of Cipriani After-School Care, with four program sites located in Belmont, California, 25 miles south of San Francisco. Karen is a National AfterSchool Association (NAA) accreditation endorser, a California School-Age Consortium (CalSAC trainer) and is on the Bay Area Chapter Board of CalSAC. In her free time, she can be found creating beautiful glass bead necklaces, enjoying family life, travel and the occasional shopping trip.

Michele Cogley continues to teach within the San Francisco Unified School District, works closely with the school's after-school program, and enjoys her children and grandchildren and the life living in the San Francisco Bay Area provides.

Lori Ottolini Geno lives in San Francisco and is a consultant working with programs on a range of topics, program management, quality, curriculum, literacy and math, and behavior guidance to name a few. Lori is the President of the Bay Area Chapter of CalSAC, serves on the Child Development Committee of the San Francisco Psychoanalytic Institute, and still finds time to be with her family, cook, read good books, travel, get out into nature and, occasionally, make handmade paper bowls.

From left: Michele Cogley, Karen Haas-Foletta, and Lori Ottolini Geno

Table of Contents

Author's Notes:

Karen: When I wrote the first edition of this book, I was pregnant with my son Nicholas. Many changes have occurred, both personally and professionally, since the book was published in 1990. Colleagues throughout the years asked me when I would write a new book and I replied, "Time is hard to come by," being a full-time working mother of two boys. In January 1999, I left West Portal C.A.R.E., Inc. in San Francisco to be the Executive Director of Cipriani After-School Care, Inc. and to consult. When I began as the Director of West Portal C.A.R.E. in 1985, it was one small site. When I left there were five sites serving over 450 children and youth, an example of how very quickly our field is growing!

When my oldest son entered kindergarten, the elementary school down the block re-opened and I was selected to provide the on-site child care. I opened Cipriani After-School Care, now serving 100 children and one of four program sites. I work full time at Cipriani and continue with writing projects, quality improvement training, workshops and accreditation.

I took the time recently to re-read this book with an update in mind. Two things were immediately obvious. The first is that much of the practical information in the original book and the "hands-on" activities are still applicable today. Most of those sections have not been significantly changed.

The second is that the field of caring for children and young people in their out-of-school time has changed dramatically. In 1988, most politicians had little understanding of what school-age care was. Today politicians not only know what it means, but they are writing bills, funding national and local projects, and using school-age child care as campaign platforms! This public awareness of our field has happened because of many efforts. Individual child care professionals have let their voices be heard. National leadership in the field of school-age care has been provided by the National Institute for Out-of-School Time (NIOST), funded since 1979; School-Age NOTES, a national resource organization established in 1980; the National School-Age Care Alliance, now the National AfterSchool Association (NAA), formed in 1987; and The Afterschool Alliance, dedicated to raising awareness of the importance of after-school programs, advocacy and the host of "Lights On After-School." These organizations provide written materials, training, technical assistance, and advocacy. Many states have school-age care affiliates advocating for school-age care on the local level.

Few books and resources for school-age care professionals were available in 1989. Our book was one of the first published and it has continued to sell steadily over the years. Individual programs use it as a resource and colleges use it as a textbook. Today many good resources, publications, research reports and organizations are available and the updated bibliography reflects these changes.

In the first edition, when we talked about meeting the needs of older children in after-school programs it usually meant third, fourth or fifth graders. Now there is a need to provide quality programs for middle-school youth. I have developed two successful programs for middle-school youth, and for the past several years have served on committees organizing a yearly national conference devoted to planning and implementing programs for this population. In order to share some insights into working with this very challenging age group, there is a new section about middle-school programming.

The original book stated that recruiting and retaining qualified, experienced staff members who meet the needs of school-age children are major concerns. Low pay, part-time hours and lack of recognition make it difficult for concerned personnel to stay committed. Unfortunately, this statement still holds true today. Therefore, a section about staff recruitment and retention has also been added.

I hope you enjoy the new version of *School-Age Ideas and Activities for After-School Programs*. I would welcome any comments. You can reach me via email, Khaasfolet@aol.com.

Michele: When this book was originally published, I was involved in after-school care daily, my children were still living at home and I was the Assistant Director of West Portal C.A.R.E., Inc. In 1990 I became a 3rd -5th grade classroom teacher at John Muir Elementary School in San Francisco, a culturally and linguistically diverse, low performing, inner-city school.

I spent four years in the innovative City Science Program started by Dr. Bruce Alberts and continued to be involved in a Systemic Change program. I participated in National Geographic Society's training program for urban teachers and in 1998 was part of an advanced leadership-training program. Geography proved to be a vital discipline that has permeated my teaching and perspective. Our Geo Team presents training and institutes locally and statewide, combining literature, movement, science, art, social studies, math and geography. It was an opportunity to combine my three favorite subjects, science, geography and literature. In addition to those experiences, responding to the needs of Our students, I became part of the pilot program for the California Reading and

Literature Project — Reading Results, training for both K-3 and 4-6.

Through the years, I have been a mentor teacher, educator and presenter in several subjects, always with a focus on integrating whenever possible. My experiences have provided a unique perspective on after-school care. Classroom teachers see daily the effects of each child's after-school situation. It is essential for children to have safe, caring, supportive, creative and challenging places to go after school. There is a unique purpose for the after-school environment. The professionalism, concern and enthusiasm of people who provide that care are of utmost importance.

A crucial element is cooperation and communication between parents, the school staff, and after-school caregivers. It is important to have connections between the child's worlds. It is meaningful for classroom teachers to be invited to an outside event and for students to have classroom teachers attend. It is valuable for regular school staff to be asked to participate in tutoring or enrichment classes in the after-school programs also. Classroom teachers and after-school care professionals need to take time to talk to and support each other, to share their knowledge and programs, especially when those ideas might provide opportunities for growth for a child, or support for a family.

Lori: From being the accidental, college student child care worker in the mid-1970's to a consultant working with programs and staff on the issues of professionalism, advocacy and program quality, my journey has been filled with many experiences, some profound, many inspiring, along with the occasional frustrating experience thrown in to keep me on my toes. Through it all, I have had the honor to work with and learn from the best the field has to offer and I thank everyone I have met on my extraordinary journey. You have helped me to be deliberate and intentional in my work, given me the clarity to understand what children and youth need to be healthy, provided me the opportunity to learn the value of good supervision and management and learn how critical professional development is to the quality of a program.

I continue to live in San Francisco and often find my work taking me throughout California, where I have the unique opportunity to see the myriad of programs available and to meet and work with the people who make up this wonderful field.

Ideas

Program Schedule

Staff Recruitment & Retention

Room Environment & Arrangement

Multicultural Curriculum

Quality Program Standards

Family Communication

Professional Growth & Development

Middle School

Behavior Guidance

Interest Clubs

Age Grouping

Conflict Resolution

Academic Enhancement & Support

Significance of Play

Introduction

Caring for school-age children during their out-of-school hours is a profession requiring a unique mix of skills and abilities on the part of the adult leaders. This book is for the directors and staff of school-age care and youth development programs who work in before-and-after-school programs, summer and recreational programs, and child care and educational programs.

As we talked with numerous professionals involved in school-age care, it became clear there is a demand for a practical, straightforward, age-appropriate information and activity guide. As directors of out-of-school programs, we have used the ideas, suggestions and activities in this book successfully for many years. Our ideas come from a variety of sources, including books and magazines, conferences, workshops, university course work, other child care professionals, and from real life experiences. Activities which are "old standards" are included because school-age children still enjoy them.

The State of Our Profession

In 1988, when the first edition of this book was being written, the field of school-age care (SAC) was becoming more commonplace in communities throughout the United States due to changing family needs. The field was new and a provider of school-age care often was not recognized as a professional whereas preschool as a profession was becoming more recognized. School-age care was a more scattered, unorganized, and isolated profession. Since that time the field has developed a national organization, the National AfterSchool Association (NAA) – formerly the National School-Age Care Alliance (NSACA). Standards of quality have been established and a program accreditation system developed. The benefits of after-school programs have been researched and widely disseminated to the public, however; some challenges remain a part of the profession.

Challenges in Our Profession

Recruiting and retaining qualified, experienced staff who meet the needs of school-age children and youth continues to be a concern. Barriers to attracting qualified staff include:

- low pay
- part-time hours and split-shifts
- a lack of public and professional recognition

Limitations in training, support and professionalism in the field continue to frustrate many providers. Colleges have acknowledged the growth in the after-school field, expanding the number of specific and related courses devoted to educating school-age care professionals. In many communities colleges still only offer early childhood education courses. Some colleges have courses where students can receive a Bachelor's Degree or credential in school-age and youth development, such as Concordia University in Minnesota.

Limited Funding

Limited funding will always be a challenge to the after-school field. Sources of support for SAC programs range from 21st Century Community Learning Center grants to state programs such as California's After School Education and Safety Program. There has been an increase in latchkey funding and local government initiatives that set aside a percentage of the budget to child care. Private foundations, realizing the importance of out-of-school programming, have also increased their support of after-school services – both directly to programs and indirectly, through larger professional support organizations, initiatives, and private funding to programs. Many programs survive through the payment of fees for services, with little or no additional support.

School-age programs differ tremendously depending on population, numbers of children, space, facility and type of program, staff and leadership. Despite these differences, people who work with children share the ultimate goal of helping children develop to their fullest potential. To assist and support this effort are active professional groups and organizations in almost every state. These professional groups, which are, for the most part, affiliated with the National AfterSchool Association, provide support services, mentoring, professional development and training, technical assistance and advocacy to SAC programs. Professional development for SAC staff, increased public awareness of the need, and advocacy in local and state governments are a part of the continuing work of school-age care professionals.

The Voice of Experience

In our program there is a Director, an Assistant Director who is second in charge, Head or Lead Teachers, teachers and teachers' aides.

What to Call Ourselves

Throughout this book, you will note many names are used to describe the adults who care for school-age children during their out-of-school hours. The licensing agency in California defines school-age care providers as teacher/director, teachers and aides. In some states, providers are not titled "teacher" unless they have a credential and work in academic classrooms.

Being considered and valued as a professional is very important. School-age caregivers are not baby sitters, nor are they custodial care providers. We feel strongly that while we are not teachers in a formal academic sense, and our curriculum is not strictly adult-directed, we teach and guide children and provide learning opportunities on a variety of topics and important concepts. We have decided to use the title "teacher" throughout this text. We also use the title "adult leader," "staff member," "caregiver," "group leader," "youth leader," "counselor" and "child care professional."

Richard Scofield, founder of School-Age NOTES, once stated, "We may continue to call our individual programs and job titles by different names. However, let us declare ourselves and band together as professionals who care for and about school-agers."*

Philosophy

Children spend many hours in out-of-school care. In this "home away from home" setting great growth and development can and does occur. With the amount of time spent in out-of-school care, children need to develop a sense of belonging in their care facility. The safety of the children is critical. Structure and limits are necessary. Clearly posted safety rules, which children help develop, aid children, staff and families to know what is expected. It is essential that

*Scofield, Richard. "What's in a name???"*School-Age NOTES,* Vol. IX, May/June 1989, p.2.

rules are enforced consistently and that children know the consequences. Many school-age children equate limits with a sense of security and caring. If children feel safe and secure, they will feel free to constructively select and pursue activities that challenge and interest them.

Choice of activities should be a central part of out-of-school care programs. The children's diverse needs, interests and developmental levels must be addressed when planning and implementing curriculum. The environment should be designed to be challenging, both mentally and physically, to foster independence, and to allow children to grow and develop at their own pace.

Family and community contributions, as well as that of the children, to program content are vital. While the mission and philosophy of the program set the foundation, the program should reflect the interests of the children. Parents and guardians want to know their concerns for their children are being met. SAC professionals offer valuable experience; however, their role is primarily that of facilitator. It is their responsibility to strive to meet the needs of the group, while addressing individual needs of the children and families.

An essential ingredient to a successful program is a well-rounded and responsive staff. School-agers do not want staff to treat them like preschoolers, nor do they want the same academic structure as the school. To be effective and appropriate, staff must be willing to adapt and expand their knowledge base. Professional development, training and education in many areas contribute to a well-rounded staff. These areas include: recreation, physical education, child and adolescent development, science, cooking, environmental science, and visual and performing arts.

A successful SAC program is one with a vision, mission and philosophy, which is visible daily. Programs must be intentional and deliberate in providing services for children, youth and their families.

How People Learn

By understanding how humans learn, a teacher can develop and implement a more interesting, varied and enriching program, a program that provides a variety of opportunities to engage children on a variety of levels. This understanding gives you a solid base for diversifying activities in a program and helps provide individualization in a group setting for the many ways in which children learn. One useful resource is Howard Gardner's Theory of Multiple Intelligences. Gardner defines eight intelligences of humans:

- **Logical-Mathematical** – Uses numbers and reasoning effectively, follows traditional teaching practices, using observation and experimentation and responds well to "what if" type questions.

  Child Likes To: Ask questions, explore patterns and relationships, do experiments, figure things out and solve problems, engage in classification activities, play strategy games and use computers and technology.

  You Can Try: Creating codes, diagrams, graphs and charts, mapping, logic and word games, debates, research projects, and computers, internet and email.

- **Verbal Linguistic** – Uses words effectively, whether orally or in writing and effectively absorbs information by listening, reading, speaking and writing.

  Child Likes To: Read, write and listen, tell stories, rhymes, riddles and tongue twisters, play verbal memory games or word games and give presentations.

  You Can Try: Oral and written word games, journals or script writing, oral presentation, peer tutoring, group discussions, debates, talking books, computers and reading aloud.

- **Musical** – Perceives, creates and expresses musical forms, recognizes sounds and remembers melodies and recognizes tonal patterns.

Child Likes To: Sing, hum and/or whistle tunes, play musical instruments, listen to and respond to music, use movement or signing to convey information and listen to music while studying.

You Can Try: Composing music, musical presentations, listening to a variety of music, making instruments and music software.

- **Naturalist** – Discriminates among living things, sensitive to the natural world, recognizes and classifies natural objects.

  Child Likes To: Take nature walks, be outside in nature, collect and classify things, care for living things and engage in hands-on nature experiences.

  You Can Try: Nature walks, gardening, recycling and environmentalism, nature centers, nature books and journaling, outdoor activities, programs on animals and collections.

- **Spatial**- Perceives the visual-spatial world accurately, exhibits sensitivity to color, line, shape, form, space and their relationships and visualizes and graphically represents ideas.

  Child Likes To: Put things together and take them apart, engage in art projects, design and build things, look at pictures, slides, movies and daydream and visualize.

  You Can Try: Charts, graphs, computer graphics and construction, visual art projects, manipulatives, puzzles and mazes, videos, slides, movies and picture books.

  - **Interpersonal** – Perceives and makes distinctions in the moods, intentions, motivations and feelings of other people; operates primarily through person-to-person relationships.

    Child Likes To: socialize with peers, have many friends, help others, mediate conflicts, organize activities, and work on cooperative projects.

You Can Try: Circle times, community involvement, co-operative groups, interactive software or email, board games, leadership roles, peer tutoring and role-plays.

- **Intrapersonal** – Has an accurate understanding of one's own self, is aware of inner moods, intentions and motivations and has capacity for self-discipline, self-understanding and self-esteem.

     Child Likes To: Work alone, follow own instincts, be original, engage in self-paced, self-selected and individualized activities, express self in own unique style and reflect, "Think about thinking".

     You Can Try: Goal setting, reflection time, journals, problem solving, self-directed learning and private space.

- **Bodily Kinesthetic** – Uses whole body to express ideas and feelings, facility in using hands to produce or transform things, relates to physical movement and wisdom about the body and bodily motion.

     Child Likes To: Engage in hands-on active learning, gross and fine motor activities, move, touch and explore environment; use body language, gesture and touch, dance, drama, role play and tactile experiences; hear and tell stories and move, twitch, fidget while sitting still.

     You Can Try: Graphing physical activities, designing models, manipulatives, role plays, drama, performing arts, scavenger hunts, tactile activities, puppetry and maps.

Significance of Play

Play is an important component of a child's life. It is a child's way of life from infancy to about age eight. Learning to play builds the foundation for life as an adult. Play is the most natural way for a child to grow, use his-her capacities and learn a variety of skills. Make sure to include many opportunities for play in your programs. Do not limit play opportunities only to younger children – children and youth (as well as adults!)

of all ages need time to play. Frank and Theresa Caplan suggest some of the benefits of play in their book *The Power of Play**:

- Providing time for play supports growth, giving a child an opportunity to imitate, explore and test ideas.

- Play is a voluntary activity. By giving children self-choice in play, you are building confidence in their power and decision-making abilities.

- Play provides an imaginary world where the world becomes manageable, giving a child the opportunity for mastery, understanding and problem solving.

- Play offers the opportunity for growth and development in a child's physical coordination, agility and body control.

- Play offers children freedom of action, with opportunities for trial and error.

- Play is important in building interpersonal relationships and skills.

- Play provides a base for language building by providing opportunities to learn many of the skills needed for reading mastery.

- Play helps children further interests and concentration; it helps to build and expand willpower and attention span.

- Play is the way children investigate the material world and evokes imaginative and creative learning.

- Play helps children learn adult roles, helping children understand and become aware of what people do.

- Play helps to clarify a child's thoughts, refining their judgment skills and understanding.

*Caplan, Frank with Caplan, Theresa. *The Power of Play*. New York: Anchor Press/ Doubleday. 1974.

A Chance to be Children

Children's lives today are often hurried and over scheduled. Some parents and guardians fill their children's free time with activities and put pressure upon them to succeed. They are rushed from one endeavor to another, given little opportunity to be themselves to discover their interests and talents. There is a tendency for parents, teachers, peers, the media, and society in general to encourage children to grow up quickly. Children are frequently pushed past their important childhood years into the adult world. They are encouraged to assume adult values toward clothing, sports, responsibilities, academics, adult problems, boy/girl relations and commitment to future goals.

There is no direct way to control the flow of adult-type information into children's lives, but there are ways to help them find time to grow more naturally and at their own pace. Make your program the environment where those hurried and pushed children can slow their pace. Permit children to find the time to have fun, relax, create, hang out, talk, share, explore and just be kids. Let children even find the time to be "bored." Dr. David Elkind, the author of *The Hurried Child**

says that it is good for children to be bored, because then they have to go into themselves for their own resources. These days, too many children do not have a chance to reflect. After-school programs are a perfect place for these moments of self-exploration to occur.

Academic Enhancement and Support

- After-school programs can support the development of the academic skills necessary for children/youth to be successful students.

---

* Elkind, David, PhD. *The Hurried Child*. Cambridge: Perseus Publishing. 2001.

- Staff can creatively integrate state or national curriculum content standards in fun, engaging and interesting out-of-school activities.
- Knowing the content of the school-day curriculum helps staff plan appropriately in providing academic opportunities, enhancement and support.
- The out-of-school program can provide opportunities for children and youth to participate in hands-on activities and provide the time for greater discovery and learning not available in the academic day.

State or federally-supported or mandated after-school programs, often located in schools, are primarily designed to provide enrichment and academic support. These programs are often at schools which are "low performing" on standardized tests. Many of these programs were funded with the expectation that after-school academics would help raise targeted students' test scores. The aim is  for these after-school programs to function as extensions and enhancements to the school day, and involve family, community organizations, school staff, and district programs.

There are usually three components included in the goals for this type of program: academic, enrichment and personal growth. Individual tutoring for specific skill needs and homework support are a part of the academic component along with reading and math programs, science and technology activities, social studies, art and music. The enrichment component includes what traditionally have been recreational program activities: visual and performing arts, crafts, team sports, cooking, dance, field trips. The personal growth component involves activities that help children to make strong and constructive personal choices and work together cooperatively within group situations. Personal growth activities are designed to develop life skills, including (but not limited to) nutrition and health, violence and gang prevention, conflict resolution, inclusion and diversity training. These activities often involve partnerships with the school and community outreach programs.

Scheduling is a serious consideration for academic programs. Program staff needs to make realistic and aware decisions about the amount of homework that the program is going to accommodate. This time decision needs to be made by taking into account the parents' expectations, classroom teachers' concerns, and the program staff's need to provide a well-rounded program for students. Parents often expect that children will finish all homework in the after-school time, unaware that there are many more aspects to what the program is offering. Care needs to be taken that homework does not become the all-encompassing focus for the program, and that school staff and parents are kept well informed about the other components in the program, and the program's focus.

Staff Recruitment and Retention

It has become increasingly difficult for after-school programs to hire quality staff and to retain them. Most school-age care jobs are part-time and those who need full-time employment are looking for jobs with preschools or in other industries.

Programs have had to develop new strategies to recruit new staff. Where in the past ads in local papers used to be the best source to find new employees, other sources have become as effective. The internet has expanded to include opportunities for posting available positions, reaching a broader range of potential candidates.

Some strategies that have worked well to recruit staff:

1. Create flyers to post throughout the community including junior colleges, four-year universities, religious centers, community centers, senior citizen centers, at popular retail clothing stores, juice bars, coffee bars and bookstores.

2. Advertise on the internet, in local papers, on college job boards and on local access television.

3. Word of mouth works very well! Ask your families to spread the word. Give staff members finder fees for word-of-mouth hires.

The Voice of Experience

In the past, we've been careful when placing an ad in a local paper to never give out the telephone number of our program. Today the phone number, fax number and e-mail address are included to make it easier for applicants to contact the organization. The salary range is often not included in the advertisement to give flexibility to meet the salary expectations of qualified candidates. Care is taken to include the location of the program and the hours of employment because many are not willing to commute long distances and/or do not want to work part-time.

4. Go to your local high school child development classes and request to speak to the class.

5. Get to know the job placement personnel at your local high school and colleges.

6. Work with state organizations that provide training for those entering the work force.

7. Go to college job fairs or other job fairs in your community.

8. Advertise through local child care resource and referral agencies and child care and Cooperative Extension organizations.

9. Locate national organizations for people relocating to your area.

10. Advertise with local volunteer groups.

11. Contact organizations for retired and semi-retired professionals from related fields.

Once staff are hired, it is critical to find ways to retain them. Many programs rely on college students as their employee pool. Many of these employees stay with a program for one to two years. These realities can create an environment of "revolving door" staff in programs. With these difficulties in mind, program directors can cultivate long-term staff members by creating opportunities for growth within the organization.

Some strategies to retain staff:

1. Provide the best pay and benefits possible. Merit increases whenever possible, at least annually, should be built into the program budget. Create the best benefit package possible within financial limitations. Benefits should include mandated federal and state requirements, health benefits, life insurance, paid sick and vacation leave. Offering benefits to employees working less than full-time can help you retain staff even if you cannot offer full-time employment. Free or reduced child care costs, matching funds for retirement plans and education reimbursement are also benefits offered by programs.

2. Provide a comprehensive orientation for all new staff. A thorough orientation is the start of a good on-going professional development and training program. Provide on-going staff training through staff meetings, conferences and workshops as much as the budget will allow. Arrange for staff to attend local and, if possible, national training events. Scholarships are often available through a number of organizations. Conferences and workshops are great forums for staff to share their skills and expertise. A regular staff meeting that includes a training component should be an integral part of a program. Some programs have staff meetings daily, others weekly and some programs meet monthly. If staff meetings are outside of regular work hours, it is required by law to pay staff for attending. If meetings are in the evening provide dinner. Reward staff for attending workshops and training events with merit increases in salary. Acknowledge participation in the program newsletter.

3. Evaluate new employees at regular intervals. Provide a probation period for new employees. Evaluating at the three-month mark provides early incentive and helps the director and employee set goals, recognize strengths, and evaluate performance to date. If possible, provide a small merit increase at this time. Schedule formal evaluations with each employee annually.

4. Provide an educational fund that rewards staff monetarily for taking additional courses and workshops related to their daily work.

5. Create an environment that expects professional growth and development from the staff and provide upward movement opportunities within the organization.

6. Include the staff in assessing training needs. Bring in outside resources available in the community on a wide range of topics. Sometimes these workshops can be done for very little cost; more than one program can share the cost of the training opportunities.

7. Use peer resources and mentoring: Sharing skills, expertise and talents in a program help improve staff morale and can help retain staff and improve the level of quality.

8. Acknowledge and reward staff by recognizing good work with verbal praise, written acknowledgment and evaluation. These are good tools for increasing a sense of self-worth, professionalism and retention of employees.

9. Recognize staff birthdays and life events with small gifts, time off work, a dinner or lunch at a restaurant, a card from the children or any other way to remember them. Some programs have families donate money or gift certificates that are given to the staff. Other programs ask local businesses for their support. Include recognitions for accomplishments in your newsletters to families.

Professional Growth and Development

One of the most important components of a successful program is the quality of the staff. A solid foundation of any school-age program includes staff that is well qualified and well supervised. One of the most significant aspects of the program administrator's job is to be sure that the expectations for staff are met so that they are equipped, able, and confident to provide the best care possible for children and youth.

Professional development and training should be made available to staff on a regular basis in a well-planned and organized manner. Staff receiving on-going professional development and training will be able to offer a more comprehensive and engaging program to the children/youth. Some of the topics and training areas to include in a training program:

- child and youth assessment
- ways of working with school-age children and youth
- health and safety
- planning program activities
- creating school-age and after-school environments
- behavior guidance
- integrating academics and enrichment

- special needs and inclusion
- cultural diversity and awareness
- partnerships and collaboration with parents, schools and communities
- selection and supervision of program staff
- leadership development
- program evaluation
- middle-school programming

Professional development and training must be relevant and useful. Staff must be able to apply the training in their daily work. Try developing a training plan, survey staff, bring in outside trainers, collaborate with other programs or try to get college credit for training events. Make training a natural part of the program. When a staff is engaged in learning and developing, the children will also be more engaged in learning.

Family Communication

Talking to parents or guardians is often difficult for staff. Most interactions between parents and staff are brief and hurried, occurring at arrival or dismissal. Working parents often do not have a great deal of time to communicate with staff members. They are busy, tired, sometimes impatient or can be intimidated entering a large and active center. Many parents arrive near closing time; staff are also tired and ready to end their work day. This is a sensitive time of the day and requires gentle handling. It falls on staff to be professional during these moments. Some form of communication is essential when parents come to pick up their children. This can be eye contact and a smile, a tactful inquiry or assistance getting the child ready to leave.

A child who is in the middle of a project or a game may not want to leave. Teachers can help by reminding the child the parent wants to leave and he/she can continue work on the project the next day. Often this reassurance means the difference between a war of wills and peaceful coexisting. A parent in a hurry would rather not have to wait for a clean-up. However, it is important that the child does clean-up before leaving, so that the child learns to take responsibility for his or her actions. The caregiver may have to remind the parent of its importance. A few moments of transition time before going home is often necessary. If parents allow five to ten minutes for children to finish up, the results are often far more relaxed than always rushing children out the door. Caregivers can use these five minutes to assist the children, talk to the parents, or both.

Parents of kindergarten children need special consideration. Even if the child has attended preschool, both parent and child are experiencing a new process of letting go and are in the middle of an important transition. Kindergarten is often very different from preschool or child care and the behaviors and expectations frequently are more demanding for the children. They are entering an academic world and their parents are entering a new relationship with them. For some, the transition is smooth; for others, it is a rough one. Patience and calm support are beneficial for them during this year.

However, parent attachment to children is not related to age; they all have similar concerns. Working parents have special stresses, the hardest of which is the lack of time and energy for their children, and the guilt that often results. Parents with financial problems, coupled with family stress, are especially in need of extra patience from child care staff. For some working parents their only social life consists of the chats they have at the program.

Parents have a great investment in their children and most identify strongly with their successes and failures. Competent parents may have a child with behavior problems for reasons other than their parenting skills. Assistance may be necessary to put their parenting in perspective.

Perhaps the hardest thing about family communication is knowing how to describe a child's difficulties without making the parent feel it is their fault, or that they are in some way a "bad" parent. They may be sensitive about their roles as working parents and may resent the relationships that teachers develop with their children, considering how little time during the week they have to spend with them. Parents depend on child care and, consequently, often have mixed feelings about it. They may resent a teacher who does not

8 suggestions to communicate effectively with parents

1. Learn parents' names and try to greet them every time they enter the program.

2. Ask families to share information about their lifestyle – the intake or enrollment form is a good place to gather this type of information. Remember to be sensitive to and respectful of their privacy.

3. Say something positive about their child whenever possible. Creating a positive relationship first can make more difficult conversations easier later on.

4. Respect parental confidences.

5. Discuss only essential details of incidents and avoid naming other children involved whenever possible.

6. Timing is important; it takes practice and patience to learn that some things can wait.

7. In your newsletter or handbook include a section about going home and transition times. Offer suggestions and resources on issues or concerns families are facing.

8. Remember, a sense of humor is essential when working with parents and their children.

have children of his or her own because they feel that the teacher lacks the day-to-day home life experience.

When you must give more difficult or negative information to a parent about a child, approach it in a manner that will deal directly with the issue at hand, encourages partnership between you and the parent, and shows that you understand the child's temperament, personality, and ability. An example would be to say to a parent, "Alex has been hitting other children. We have been working to handle this with Alex, but we would like to include you in our conversation," instead of, "Alex is having trouble controlling his temper." Constructive support and regular communication are often necessary. Parents or guardians do appreciate a teacher's observations and suggestions and often want to share their observations and suggestions.

Children and families have a variety of needs and your program may not be the solution for every family. When a child's individual problems are so severe that they disrupt the balance and flow of the entire program, it is time to consider other possibilities. We cannot be everything to every child and family. This is a hard concept to grasp, but we must look at the good of the program as a whole. It is very difficult to ask a family to remove their child from a program, but it may be the best solution. In this case, help the family locate another program, counseling or other assistance.

What Makes A Quality Program?

Regardless of the type of program, it is important to strive for continued program quality. Children and youth do better when their out-of-school environment has a commitment to being a quality program. Components of high quality programs include:

1. *Qualified and capable staff*

- Staff is supported, staff is competent, staff is empowered so staff can then support, build and empower children and youth.

- Professional development and training is an integral part of the program. Training is relevant and useful to the staff.

- Staff is compensated to the highest degree possible by the program or organization. Compensation includes wages, full-time hours, regular schedules, medical benefits, personal time (vacation or sick), retirement or 401K plans and educational reimbursement.

- A quality program hires and retains stable and knowledgeable staff. By having a commitment to the retention of staff, the quality of a program improves.

2. *Facility, equipment, materials and activities that encourage discovery, group development, exploration and interest*

- A variety of materials and activities are provided that are age appropriate and interesting to the children and considers their ages and interests.

- Adequate facility and equipment creates a safe, healthy and engaging environment.

- Children have access to enough materials to support the number of children attending. Materials can be used and accessed regularly by the children. The activities foster a variety of group sizes and experiences, including individual activities.

3. *Effective leadership*

- Leadership is critical to manage, organize, supervise and achieve goals and outcomes. The most wonderful facility, staff and program can flounder with a lack of leadership.

- A program needs leadership that is visionary, propels the staff, children and families to realize dreams and achieve outcomes and goals.

Quality Standards

For many years, the field did not have a common language to define quality. We now have a system by which we can discuss quality, using the same language to quantify and qualify terms. One tool, the NAA's *Standards for Quality,* provides a structure, a planning tool, topics to discuss, and a measurement for improvements in all program areas. The *Standards for Quality* is a useful resource tool for thinking about program quality and program quality improvements. For a listing of the 36 keys to quality as defined in the *Standards for Quality* and other information about the NAA accreditation program, refer to the appendix at the back of this book. Below are some of the exemplary practice areas included in quality programs.

1. Vision and Ownership: Program leaders, program staff and other stakeholders (including principals, site administrators, board members and others in positions of influence) have a clear understanding and shared ownership of the program vision, mission and the principles on which the program is designed. All can articulate these in a consistent manner to others. Strong support for the program in the school and community is clearly demonstrated through words and actions. The program's vision and core principles are in practice at all program-related levels.

2. Program Leadership: An integrated system of leadership, mentorship, and management is developed focusing on helping staff to succeed. This includes:

- training and a system of coaching support,
- mechanisms to ensure positive communication, and
- shared and site-based decision-making.

3. Community Involvement: The after-school program provides activities that increase the children's knowledge of their communities and a positive sense of connection. Children and youth have opportunities to contribute or "give back" to their communities through program activities. The program engages parents and community members as vital resources to enrich the program by providing opportunities to become involved and support the program in various ways.

4. Asset Development: The after-school staff is trained in asset development principles and staff uses them to shape their program structure and staff practices. Activities are intentionally designed to support key developmental experiences for children and youth, and feedback from program participants is used to assess and improve program quality.

5. Safety: The program provides a sense of physical safety and emotional safety with the surrounding adults and peers. They know:

- they will be protected from harm;
- the program rules to ensure individual safety will be fairly and consistently enforced by supervising adults; and
- they will be respected and valued by others, regardless of cultural and/or personal differences.

The program staff have reviewed issues of physical and emotional safety together and adjusted the program to deepen the sense of safety of program participants.

6. Supportive Relationships: The program is intentionally structured to build positive and supportive relationships between children and adults and among the children themselves. Children and youth can identify adults they can go to for support or guidance and feel that the staff know them as individuals. Staff are trained in the skills necessary to build a sense of relationship and community. There is a process in place to address differences among participants and to resolve conflicts in positive ways.

7. Learning and Skill-Building: Opportunities are provided to build new skills through learning experiences that are both challenging and interesting. Learning activities are aligned to children and youth's interests and draw upon strategies to fully engage and motivate children and youth as active learners.

8. Academic Alignment: School-day staff and after-school staff work together to ensure that after-school academic components (including homework and educational enrichment) are aligned with the regular school day. On-going staff development and training result in an environment where participants demonstrate enthusiasm for learning, and help encourage and support academic success.

9. Youth Participation: The program empowers children and youth to participate in meaningful ways by:

- promoting the development and practice of leadership skills,
- offering opportunities for participation in decision making, and
- offering opportunities for input on the program design and on-going activities.

Staff is trained in youth leadership strategies and practices that promote increased participation.

10. Attendance: Children and youth are attending the program regularly because they are offered interesting, engaging, and relevant activities. Families are also interested in sending their children and youth to the program regularly because of the benefits they see the program offers their child.

11. Measuring Outcomes: There is a system in place for measuring and managing outcomes. This is part of a larger on-going improvement process, which relies on data to identify areas of strength and those needing further development. Programs develop and implement plans to modify organizational structures and worker practices to improve program outcomes.

12. Sustainability: The program has achieved a diversified balance of funding that allows for growth and significantly increases the program's chances for long-term sustainability.

Behavior Guidance

During the course of the day program staff must work with the wide variety of behaviors of the children. Due to the ages and developmental stages of the children and youth, their social and emotional well being may cause behaviors that confound and frustrate staff. It is also natural that children and youth will test the limits set for them as a means to find out if the staff will keep them safe. Some important points to keep in mind:

- Staff must understand that behavior has meaning. Staff should observe for patterns in children and youth behavior that can help identify possible causes when problems occur and find effective ways to deal with the problems.

- Staff must use observation as a means to understand a child's behavior. The observations of the entire staff can help understand a child's behavior and actions and help define a course of action.

- Staff must know the children and youth enrolled in the program, be familiar with family history, the child or youth's experience during their academic day and how the child or youth interacts socially with peers and staff.

- Staff needs to create an environment that is safe, consistent and provides continuity. Many times, a child's challenging behaviors can be addressed through the environment. Schedule, room arrangement, activities offered, snack, interactions with peers and adults and children's health or well being can affect behavior.

- School-age staff must be aware that each child or youth is an individual with unique needs, abilities and interests.

- Staff need to be skilled in problem-solving techniques and understand that the "one shoe fits all" solution does not always work. There are strategies staff can learn about problem solving, individualizing and creating continuity and consistency. Staff should carefully determine who owns the problem and who or what is causing the problem.

- Staff must understand their job is to guide rather than manage so that the child or youth can learn the skills necessary for life beyond the program. Staff should help a child or youth learn to make good choices about their behavior and to assist them in identifying the problem, generating options for resolving the problem and choosing ways to help each child get his or her needs met. When a child makes a poor choice, staff use the opportunity as a means to help the child discover new options and ways to handle the same problem better.

- Staff should be familiar with and utilize several behavior guidance techniques. Staff should work to build skills, build self-esteem and confidence and help to develop life-skill strategies for dealing with conflict, choice making and day-to-day living.

- Staff should have resources available to help deal with behaviors that are far more challenging than everyday-type behaviors. These resources should include training, mental health consultation, community resources, books and each other.

Conflict Resolution

Conflict resolution in after-school programs is the process of mediation between children not getting along in a way that helps them learn to think situations through for themselves. Teachers can intervene, but often this delays resolving the problem or leaves it unresolved for the children. Children need help learning effective ways to deal with conflict and learning to decide which idea is the most constructive and useful at the time.

School-age children generally fall into one of two stages: the "Scratch my back and I'll scratch yours" stage or the "Rules are rules and that's that" stage. Younger children are usually willing to compromise if they get something out of it in return. Older children are more often set on "the way it is supposed to be for everyone," and inconsistency can be intolerable for them. Adult leaders can help children through these stages by use of conflict resolution strategies.

There are five stages to focus on during conflict resolution:

1. **Stop the conflict.**

   Calm the children down. Separate if necessary. If there has been physical injury, tend to the hurt first. When the children are calm, continue. Sit between them if they are still very angry.

2. **Define the specific problem.**

   This means listening carefully to all the children involved as they each describe what happened. Concentrate on identifying the specific problem. "She's mean to me" is not specific enough. Make sure the children elaborate and describe. "I had it first and she took it" or "She says I have to do her homework or she won't be my friend." Try to assess the source of the main conflict without judging or criticizing. Make comments that help define the problem such as, "I see, you both want to play with the ball."

3. Have children generate solutions.

Help the children come up with ideas about how to change the situation, how to fix it or what they could have said or done differently. Get ideas from all of the children involved. Do not stop when one idea sounds good; collect a few. Asking, "What else?" is a handy tool. It is difficult, but be careful not to suggest ideas yourself. Children will often have angry ideas first. Continue until they move beyond the anger; remember not to judge their ideas. "I could hit her." "Yes, you could, what else could you do?"

4. Evaluate the solution.

When there are several ideas suggested, it is time to evaluate them. Repeat their ideas back to them without critical comment and then ask what would happen next in each case. "You said you could hit her. What would happen then?" "What will happen if you do not do your homework?" Go through all the ideas and suggestions and let the children tell you what the consequences of their suggestions might be. They may say, "She'd hit me back," or, "I'd get a time out."

5. Choose and act on a solution.

Help the child or children decide on the solution that sounds best. Then help them plan how to proceed.

This process works. It can be an effective teaching and learning tool. However, it can also lead to over-verbalization and wordiness by the adult. Avoid long speeches and keep the resolution time as brief as possible. However, make sure you allow appropriate time to resolve the conflict. You are helping the children learn valuable life skills. Children are often anxious to put something behind them and move on with their routine. Adults are sometimes slower to recognize the children's need to put an incident behind them and to continue playing.

The generation of ideas and the evaluation process are important parts of conflict resolution and problem solving. Encourage children's thinking and analyzing skills whenever possible.

Multicultural Curriculum

In planning a multicultural curriculum, look at the population the program serves, the community in which the program exists and the United States as a whole. Explore the cultural background of the staff. Every society or group has its own manner of doing things, including traditions, customs, practices, philosophy, behavior, language, communication, clothing and celebrations. This creates culture and it is learned rather than genetic. The culture that people grow up in tends to influence them strongly in areas such as child rearing practices, family roles, socialization patterns, values and religious beliefs.

Louise Derman-Sparks' book, *Anti-Bias Curriculum: Tools for Empowering Young Children** shares a very exciting approach toward the topic. "Anti-bias curriculum embraces an educational philosophy as well as specific techniques and content. It is value based: Differences are good; oppressive ideas and behaviors are not. It sets up a creative tension between respecting differences and not accepting unfair beliefs and acts." Derman-Sparks believes most multicultural curricula have a positive goal, teaching children about other cultures, but do not address the important issues of everyday life in these cultures in the context of living in America. She calls this a "tourist curriculum," based solely on studies of holidays, household items and foods. She writes, "Tourist curriculum is both patronizing, emphasizing the 'exotic' differences between cultures, and trivializing, dealing not with the real-life daily problems and experiences of different people, but with surface aspects of their celebrations and modes of entertainment." Her book gives guidance as to how to implement an anti-bias curriculum and includes activities, curriculum and information about involving parents. The book also addresses sexism and bias based on disability or gender.

Suzanne Dame, a Native American child advocate, states the three most important aspects of teaching children about another culture is

---

*Derman-Sparks, Louise. *Anti-Bias Curriculum: Tools for Empowering Young Children*. Washington, DC: NAEYC. 1989.

respect, accuracy and authenticity. For example, she does not feel children should "play at being Indians" as if being an Indian is an occupation. Playing at being any ethnicity is disrespectful. Children need to learn to respect cultural differences and explore similarities.

Built within a culture are biases or prejudices about other cultures. When developing a multicultural curriculum, discovery and discussion of staffs' cultural bias or prejudice is important. Staff must talk about varying life styles, time concepts, and the values and beliefs of each staff member. Staff must know who they are and feel pride in their own cultural background before they are ready to assist children in learning about their own and other cultures.

Families are integral in developing a multicultural curriculum and should be included in the planning process. This is best accomplished through newsletters, parent meetings, informal conversations with individual parents or group discussions. Parents, guardians and extended families are excellent resources for activities, information and experiences. Ask families to contribute items from their culture, share stories, recipes and folklore.

Holidays provide a good opportunity to begin teaching children about their own and other cultural experiences. However, holidays should not become the focus of the multicultural curriculum. When choosing what holidays to incorporate into a curriculum, think about:

- The holidays the families in the program celebrate and what special preparations, activities and ceremonies are involved.

- Providing the children with a historically accurate background about the holiday.

- Respecting every holiday equally and not treating one holiday as "exotic" and another as commonplace.

- Finding commonalities with other cultures and holidays that have already been studied or for which staff and children have personal experience.

- Being aware that certain family beliefs do not allow participation in particular holiday celebrations. If this exists in the program, work with the families in creating acceptable alternatives for the child while the holiday observance is happening.

- Remembering that some families may find certain holidays stressful because of increasing commercialization, financial expectations and family obligations.

When planning curriculum in school-age programs:

- Expose children to a variety and balance of multicultural activities.

- Make multicultural activities an ongoing part of everyday curriculum.

- Take the time to present a balanced curriculum. Instead of a whirlwind "tour," focus on one specific area of interest or commonality.

- Integrate activities throughout the learning centers or interest areas; stimulate learning through the children's senses and various learning modalities.

- Have a variety of items from each culture available for regular use. Include books, games, pictures, photographs, posters, dolls, music, musical instruments and puzzles, food and clothing.

- Reflect different ethnicities with art materials such as brown, black and tan paper, skin tone crayons and collage materials.

- Invite specialists, performers and members of the community to share and present activities and information.

- Use community resources to obtain items to incorporate in your curriculum.

- Use the internet, libraries, videos, slides, photographs and magazines to create visual images.

- Make connections to other cultures you have studied. Compare, contrast and make connections. Give children opportunities to take time to learn about cultures.

It is important that multicultural curriculum is not always about people living in other countries, but also portrays similarities and differences and the rich diversity of life in the United States.

Program Scheduling

Before arriving, school-age children have spent much of their day in controlled and structured activities. Children and youth need time out of school for exercising, socializing, eating and having opportunities to make choices. The program must include a variety of activities developed for different age levels, interests and abilities. Scheduling for after-school programs is something that is distinctive to each program. How the after-school program is set up should reflect the type of school program the children are in. For example, some schools have structured academic time at the end of the day; others have a recess time. Time constraints can also change program scheduling. If children are dismissed from school after 3:30 PM, they will need a snack right away. Make the schedule flexible; it may change from month to month or year to year according to the size, ages and the needs of the children. As much as possible the schedule should meet children's individual needs within staffing limitations.

Programs must also provide a regular homework space that includes adequate adult assistance and homework tools. Engaging the families as much as possible will help children accomplish this very important life skill. Ask families to decide if the child should work on homework at the program, what homework should be completed and how long a child should work on their homework. Abide by their requests.

Some suggestions for scheduling are:

• Allow time for kindergarten children to rest if their school day ends earlier.

• First through fifth grades do not generally need a rest, but need a transition time from school to the program. Some may want to sit and "do nothing;" some may want to lounge or read a book; some may just want to daydream.

• Outside time and physical activity is important, especially when the children first arrive. After a long day of school, many children feel the need to get out and run rather than sit for quiet activities. Others may want to sit down and get their homework done.

The Voice of Experience

We set aside a supervised time for homework Monday through Thursday. Younger children spend an average 20 to 30 minutes on homework, and older children spend 45 minutes to an hour. The homework space is available up until the end of the program day.

• Limit a group "greeting" time to ten minutes or less in order to account for all children and relay any important information that they need to know for the day. Keep group size as small as possible.

• Keep transitions to a minimum. Develop a daily program that helps children move more naturally, without the need for many transitions.

• Set snack for a time when children seem hungry. Some programs offer a "come and get it" type snack; others offer a sit-down group snack.

• Let each child help prepare and clean up snack on a rotating basis; it is a great learning experience. Additionally, set up snack in a manner that allows children to participate by pouring, spreading, cutting and mixing.

• Do homework after snack or outdoor time when the children are able to sit and focus on their homework. Older children and middle-school youth may want to do homework while eating snack. This can work with proper supervision.

• Always include at least an hour of free choice and art activities in the daily schedule.

• Try to arrange professional lessons for interested students in areas such as visual and performing arts, sports, sports teams and recreation. Many working parents or guardians appreciate this service. Keep the cost reasonable for families.

• Include the children in your schedule planning. Their input indicates their needs, interests, and helps to develop a sense of ownership which makes the schedule more successful for all.

One example of a daily schedule:

Based on a large program (50-100 children) and includes kindergarteners who attend half day of school (not all school systems have such a schedule for kindergarten.)

12:00-2:30	Kindergarten children only
12:00-12:30	Lunch (Kindergarten)
12:30-1:00	Choice play and art activities
1:00-1:30	Story time and bathroom
1:30-2:40	Rest time (Non-sleepers may get up at 2:00)
2:30-3:00	Check in & Group time (K-2nd grade)
3:00-4:00	Check in & group for 3rd-5th grade Younger children choice of inside or outside Snack is an indoor choice set up at one table and children rotate through
4:00-5:00	Homework/choice play for those without or who do not do homework (Activity clubs on Fridays instead of homework)
5:00-5:45	Activity time: art projects, science, sports, games Project clean up and parent pickup begins
5:45-6:00	Indoor quiet activities/Clean-up

Room Environment and Arrangement

Environment plays an essential role in how staff, children and youth interact. How staff, children and youth treat the space, furnishings and materials; whether children and youth feel safe; and whether staff, children and youth find the activities and materials fun and interesting are all important to understanding the powerful effect of the environment in supporting the overall goals of a SAC program. Creating an atmosphere in which children's growth and development are supported is accomplished by the way the space is arranged and managed, how materials are chosen and maintained and how interpersonal relationships are developed.

Some key concepts concerning environment:

- The way in which a facility is arranged and how space is used is a significant component of the message sent to children, youth and their families.

- The environment needs to be developmentally appropriate. School-agers need a physical environment that matches their size, energy and ability.

- Behavior is strongly affected by the environment. A well-planned environment will encourage positive behaviors.

- The program environment must be designed to facilitate staff supervision of children and youth.

- The outdoor environment is an important component of the program experience and should be carefully considered in program design.

- Program materials and equipment should be selected based on safety, developmental appropriateness and utility. The materials and equipment should reflect cultures being served and support a balanced curriculum, including literacy and reading.

- The interpersonal environment that is created in a SAC program is as important as the physical environment.

Programs With Dedicated Space

Programs that have "dedicated" space, where equipment and materials do not have to be set up and taken down each day, are very fortunate. This provides the opportunity to develop and create a responsive program structure, meeting the ever-changing needs of school-age children. Room arrangement is critical for a successful program. Arranging the environment is a dynamic process. What works one year may not prove effective in six months or the next year. When planning indoor environments, keep in mind the ages, interests and developmental levels of the children.

A common approach to room arrangement is the learning center or activity area set-up. These areas include prepared environments where children choose activities depending on their interests. There is flow from one area to the next because the environment and adult supervision promote movement. Children do not have to ask permission to be in an area of the room and they can often choose how long  to stay at a project. Thus, Maria may spend her free-play time playing a game while Jimmy may participate in several activities; both are accommodated. If a child has difficulty choosing, staff assist by verbalizing the choices available then letting the child make his or her own decision. Some programs have children rotate from one center to the next, for a set time period, which is a more teacher-directed orientation. Other centers will change or alternate moveable activity areas on a daily or weekly basis. When creating the room arrangement, there are many factors to keep in mind:

- safety factors such as clear fire exits

- traffic patterns in and around areas

- size and location of each interest area

- placement of areas, such as separating noisy activities from quiet activities

- location of areas to facilitate movement of children from one area to another

- arrangement of interest areas to allow for adequate adult supervision and visibility through the use of low shelves, see-through room dividers, bookcases, and couches

- access to sinks for art, science and cooking

- close proximity to bathrooms and drinking fountains

- sufficient storage for supplies and equipment

- flexibility to adapt to the changing needs of the children

The optimum after-school environment will include:

Quiet, Soft Area — with sofa, bean bags, carpet or rug, and books situated away from doors or high traffic patterns. It is an area for reading, quiet games, relaxing, storytelling and privacy. An old bathtub filled with pillows makes a great reading place.

Open Area for Group or Circle Time — with a rug or carpet squares, large enough to accommodate the whole group.

Large Manipulative Area — an area for construction and other fine motor skills. This area may include a complete block set (hollow as well as unit blocks), LEGO™ materials, K'NEXT™, cars, and trucks, Bristle Blocks™, flexible blocks, plastic animals, people, etc. Building manipulative materials are a very important part of play and math development.

Dress-up and Dramatic Play Area — school-age children are developing work patterns and have an interest in adult roles. They want real items such as pots, pans, dishes and tools. This area can change from a post office, to a business office, and then to a doctor's office, a shoe or clothing store or a grocery store. Place items for each theme in large, labeled boxes that can be easily stored and reused.

Game and Storage Area — include in this area a variety of games with flat surfaces for game playing, open space for floor games, puzzles and other manipulative games and activities. Make sure storage space is clearly labeled with ample space for games of different sizes and shapes. Without consistent organization, this area can become very messy. Store pieces for games and puzzles in resealable plastic bags or plastic tubs with lids. The plastic bags can be hung from a string with clothespins. Label the backs of puzzle pieces so that lost pieces can be easily returned to the correct puzzle. The area should be able to accommodate a couple of groups playing a variety of games.

Hands-on Science and Exploration — have a science table or science area accessible to the children. A shelf above the table is excellent for things to be viewed without touching. The majority of items should be "hands-on" – place them in a "discovery" area. This area can also include pictures, posters and maps. Include space for child-initiated and teacher-directed projects. (See the Science Section for more information.)

Area for Older Children – have a special designated space for the older children. This space should include a homework area including all necessary materials. (See the section on Older Children for more ideas.)

Arts and Crafts Area – include ample storage for both individual and group activities. Include easily accessible materials, always available for use by the children such as paper, crayons, tape, scissors, glue, scrap material, markers, stapler and staples, envelopes, hole punch, string, yarn and paper plates. Limit the stacks of paper to avoid waste and unnecessary mess. Use recycled paper for daily drawings, save the good paper for special projects. If you have a cubby available, create an "Art Cart," a cubby accessible to the children. Put the children in charge of cleaning and restocking the Art Cart on a weekly basis. Store special projects materials in a place available to the staff. A shelf for storing long-term or unfinished projects is desirable. A multi-sided easel with a vinyl mat underneath and a drying rack are wonderful for painting. Include an area for activities like working with clay. Plastic tablecloths are good for floor mats and table covers and are easy to wash and reuse. Good lighting and a separation from the general traffic flow is important. (See the Arts and Crafts Sections for more suggestions.)

Cubbie Area — children need a place to store their personal belongings. Traditional cubbies can be purchased or be innovative and use stacking items such as plastic crates. Include the child's name on the cubby. Remember to have the children regularly clean and straighten their cubby.

Storage Area — for supplies and equipment with items well labeled. Items that are used more frequently are accessible while specialty items are stored up and away. Regular maintenance of the area by the staff is necessary.

Cooking Area — for the preparation and storage of food and utensils.

Family Area — with sign-in/out area, mailboxes, folders storing finished artwork ready to take home and a bulletin board. Some centers have a couch or chairs in this area so adults can wait or socialize with other adults. These family areas often have reading material, health and safety information, and sometimes coffee and treats. This area should reflect the program. It should be welcoming and tell the families about the program. Families primarily see only this area of the program.

Staff Area — with staff mailboxes, a place to store belongings, a bulletin board with emergency procedures, staff log book, payroll timecards, telephone access, staff information, schedules posted, computer with internet access and a reference library. If possible, a staff lounge area is wonderful for breaks. This area can include a coffee pot, etc., comfortable chairs, and a telephone.

Programs With Shared Space

The Voice of Experience

We often purchase materials and supplies that are shared between the classroom teacher and the after-school program.

Many programs do not have dedicated space and this presents special challenges in creating a consistent, engaging and welcoming environment. However, with imagination, creativity and organization, it is possible to create, develop and operate a quality program in shared space. The key is having plenty of moveable and lockable storage units so equipment can be moved easily and safely in and out of the space. Large multi-purpose spaces can accommodate many children engaged in a variety of activities while giving a sense of warmth and intimacy, and still be set up and taken down on a daily basis. Shared classrooms can work particularly if the shared classroom serves the same age or grade during school hours, then the furniture is appropriate for the age group. If a classroom is shared, a clear understanding between the after-school staff and the classroom teacher is necessary. It takes time to develop trust and routine to make a sharing situation work well for all.

8 tips for effective shared space

1. Interest areas can still be set up on a daily basis. To define areas use tables or shelves with wheels, bulletin boards or folding storage cabinets.

2. Large pillows, bean bag chairs, pop-up tents, small folding camp chairs and small area rugs can substitute for heavier quiet-area furniture.

3. Portable signs, bulletin boards on wheels and backs of shelves can be used to define and label the learning centers and serve as room dividers.

4. Pegboard is an excellent versatile material for hanging things, making room dividers, and enclosing areas for privacy.

5. Art supplies can be stored on wheeled shelves – use containers such as baskets, large cans and tins, covered ice cream tubs or chicken buckets, and shoe boxes.

6. Removable carpet squares can be used for the quiet and group sections because they are easily stacked.

7. Plastic stackable containers on wheels work for movable cubbies.

8. The use of "spill-over space," such as a hall and special rooms, is great for doing small-group projects.

Programs with exclusive space may still, in many cases, share space. When sharing any space, develop a mutually acceptable plan with whomever the space is being shared. A good working relationship takes time and flexibility to develop. A mutually acceptable plan includes keeping the shared space neat and clean, storing belongings and daily putting the furniture back to a prescribed set up. Remember, in programs that are school-based, the school principal, secretary and janitor can make or break a program. Create a supportive relationship by communicating effectively and regularly to prevent misunderstandings.

Many programs are not allowed to put anything on the walls. To display children's artwork or put up posters, drape material, sheets, oil cloth or plastic pieces over the walls. Use heavy weight fishing line, secured at two ends, and hang the line across a wall using clothespins to display art. (Check with fire safety regulations first.) Large chalkboards, corkboards and foam boards on wheels can be purchased. Portable room dividers are available from office supply catalogs.

The Voice of Experience   What Our Program is Like

Many people ask us why our room arrangement is successful. A major reason is the low adult-child ratio (1:10) for elementary-school youth and (1:14) for middle-school youth. We have two rooms for elementary-school programs with children divided by age and developmental levels. (See the section on middle-school programs on p.60 for a glimpse of a typical program day.) Many choices are built into a structured environment. Children decide what activity to pursue. The following is a freeze-frame of what you might observe at our center during a typical, activity choice period, which is the core of our curriculum. Activity choice works for us because the planned interest areas, although often continuously changing, structure the environment.

It is 4:30 p.m. and there are 70 children present, kindergarten through fifth grade. After an outdoor time, snack and homework, it is now activity-choice time both in and out of doors.

Younger Children's Room

Dress Up – Putting on adult-sized clothing, four children are absorbed in playing house.

Large Motor Area – Three children set up the wooden train set on the rug. Two children play with LEGO™ materials at the block table. Four children build a zoo with the blocks and plastic animals.

Quiet Area – A staff member reads a storybook to four children on the couch.

Art Area – At the table six children and one teacher work with clay. Two other children cut and paste pictures and two are creating pictures of space ships.

Game Area – Two children challenge each other to mancala while two other children play chess.

Computer Area – Three children play games on the computers.

Science Table – Three butterflies, just hatching out of their cocoons, capture the attention of one six-year-old.

Older Children's Room

Quiet Area - Four children continue to work on their homework at the side table. Three children with a staff member care for the center's animals. One child, sitting on a beanbag chair, reads a book. Sprawled on the couch, two children trade cards.

Art Area - At the table six children and one teacher weave baskets. Two other children are cutting cardboard boxes to make structures.

Game Area - Two children challenge each other to a checkers game while one enjoys watching.

Computer Area - Three children work on the computers playing games, finishing homework and doing special projects. Two children have placed their names on the waiting list and watch the other children work on the computers.

Mixed-Age Group

Outside - In the play yard, 20 children are involved in various activities, including the play structure, basketball, drawing on the black top with chalk, and jump rope.

Seven staff members are strategically positioned throughout both indoor and outdoor areas.

Large Group Time / Circle Time

It is a good idea to have a time of day when all the children get together for a few minutes. This part of the day fosters group participation and a feeling of community. What this part of the program is called will vary depending on the situation and the person leading it. Many centers have an area large enough for thirty to forty children to sit at one time in a circle. This is an ideal situation and often is called "circle time," but works best with young children. Other centers have limited space for spreading out, but do have a rug area that will accommodate a similar number of children. This is usually called a "group time." The activities presented during this time will largely

depend on how much space the children have to move around and on the make-up of the group. A group with mixed ages is more challenging to control and more difficult to keep interested, but can be very exciting.

Many teachers feel uncomfortable leading a large group. Developing the skills necessary to manage a quality group takes experience, patience, and good observation skills, as well as spontaneity. Teachers often limit themselves to story reading and sharing time. While these are significant parts of an effective group time, they are not by any means all that can be done. Make group or circle time fun, interesting and diversified. The keys to a successful group or circle are timing and variety. Timing involves preplanning, using observation to spot restlessness, and the ability to shift gears if an activity is not working well. Variety means expanding the scope of group or circle time to include activities that go up, down, sideways, loud and quiet. Having the children sit in a circle is preferable for many activities such as making a spider web, doing exercises, playing musical instruments and playing games. For movement activities make sure there is enough room for children to be safe while participating. If available space limits movement, save these types of activities for times when the children can be divided into smaller groups or can be outdoors.

Music is an important part of group time. You do not need to play a musical instrument to have fun singing and doing rhythm activities with children. Older children prefer songs that are not the standard preschool type. Delightful folk songs, silly songs and even modern songs can be shared. Other group-time activities that are enjoyable are simple games, movement activities, sign-language or foreign-language learning, problem solving, program planning, dramatic activities and theme-related projects. For younger children, group time can include flannel board stories, finger plays, and tell-and-draw stories.

Many programs read story books to younger children during group time. However, older children also still love to be read to by adults. Older children may volunteer to read stories to the younger children during group time.

The Voice of Experience

In our program, the fourth and fifth graders love to have long chapter books read aloud to them. Children volunteer to give a summary of what has happened so far in the story for those who may have missed a day of reading.

6 suggestions for a successful group time

1. Vary the length, depending on the age and attention span of the children. Younger children need a shorter time. Vary the group size. Try to make your groups as small as possible so that all children can participate, listen and be heard by the staff and the group.

2. Begin group time with an activity to grab their attention and interest. Use activities that build and develop the team or group. Engage their senses. Then the group will be more able to listen or participate.

3. Pace your activities by watching the children's reactions. It is easy to tell when they are bored or restless. Change your tempo accordingly. Do not hesitate to throw out an activity that is not working. Spontaneous activities are perfectly valid.

4. Separate children who have trouble sitting next to each other before starting group time. Another way is to have an adult keep a sharp lookout for trouble. By having adults sit down with the children unobtrusively and in strategic locations many difficulties can be avoided, making it more enjoyable for everyone.

5. Allow a disruptive child to sit or draw at a nearby table rather than letting the disruption continue.

6. Do not limit group time to the indoors or the school grounds. Children need time outside each day and like to experience new places or visit old favorite ones.

Snack

When children leave their school day, many are very hungry. Snack time is an essential component of the out-of-school program. All programs must provide snack regardless of financial constraints. If your program does not serve snack due to financial constraints, contact local food banks, government agencies, public schools or restaurants, stores and bakeries in the area. Many businesses will offer free or reduced cost food to your program.

Snack should be considered an activity in and of itself. It is a great time for children to nourish themselves, interact socially and participate in a group activity. There are many ways to organize snack to provide these opportunities for children without compromising other program components. Regardless of the size or type of groups that

Resource Note: The Food Research & Action Center has published guidelines on how after-school programs, including faith-based and privately-operated programs can qualify for financial assistance to serve snacks. Go to www.frac.org for that information.

are being served snack, there are a variety of ways to make this an enjoyable time for staff and children.

Some ways to think about how to serve snack:

Buffet Style – Snack is set up buffet style. Children walk through, take snack and head to the snack-eating area. A staff person is responsible for this area. Children are responsible for cleaning their snack area, as well as to help set up and clean up the larger snack area.

Self-Service – Snack is available for a given time period. Children come, take snack and eat when they feel like it. Staff oversee this area to monitor behavior.

Snack Restaurant Table – Children come to a table, as space is available, sit and have snack. A staff person monitors the area.

Snack as a small group – A group of children, with the same daily staff person, have snack together. Snack trays or bins are prepared ahead of time and the group eats together. Depending on space, they can eat together in their small group within a larger multi-purpose space, in a designated space, or outdoors.

Social component of snack:

- Eating together is a very important life skill. Children need opportunities to sit together to practice their manners and learn how to converse while enjoying a meal together. Snack is a great time to provide this opportunity.

- Get the children involved in developing snack menus, snack preparation and set-up and clean up. Their participation in all aspects of snack builds invaluable life skills.

Preparing and cleaning up snack:

- A program needs to spend time discussing how best to accomplish the goal of both serving snack and creating a good routine for children.

- Due to time constraints many programs use a staff person to prepare and clean up snack. When possible, consider when and how you can include children in daily activities. Children find that their helpfulness is often a great way to get one-on-one attention from staff, to show off their ability and get encouragement and positive feedback from the adults.

Scheduling and routines for snack:

- Keep in mind that children and youth are hungry when they arrive after school. Do not delay snack; hunger affects behavior and one's ability to focus.

- Set up regular routines for snack, including the hygiene needs of the children and those handling food.

- Make sure you have a place to clean up and wash dishes. Have on hand adequate garbage and recycling bins. Schedule staff to share the responsibility for this component of the program.

Storing snack:

- Depending on space, you may have access to a kitchen and storage area. It is important to consider safe storage of food, safe food handling and hygiene of those setting up and cleaning up.

- A refrigerator with a freezer is an important item for a program. Many times, you can get one donated by an individual or organization. Weekly cleaning is imperative. If you share space, you may need to think about securing the refrigerator so that food does not disappear or it becomes storage for another program.

- You will need to be able to store paper goods, dry food items, fresh produce and food needing refrigeration. Cabinets or storage that are well marked for staff and organized regularly help with some of the time constraints in preparing snack.

Depending on how you choose to serve snack, you may need a variety of bins, drink containers, bowls, serving utensils, kitchen utensils. If you plan to serve heated food, please keep in mind you will need utensils for this.

The Voice of Experience

We do have an opportunity for the children to nap at our program. Each child has a cot to rest on and brings a blanket and pillow from home. A few sleep, the others rest and look at books, listen to music and stories on tape. When a child who usually sleeps does not for some reason, we can see the difference in his or her behavior as the day goes on.

Resting Kindergarten Children

If the kindergarten children come to your program for a half day, then include a rest time if possible. Many programs find it difficult to have a rest time because of space and time restrictions. However, the opportunity to have a half-hour rest time, or a one-hour nap time for those who sleep, can be genuinely beneficial. Kindergarten children tend to be very busy during school. The constant activity may be both physically and emotionally stressful, especially for the first few months. Resting provides their bodies with the much needed chance to relax and calm down. If napping is impossible, at least have the children sit down and rest, or be read to quietly.

7 hints for a successful rest time

1. Before rest time, have a group time to calm the children down and have them use the bathroom.

2. Always have the children use the same cot or mat labeled with their name on it. Have each child bring a sheet, blanket and pillow from home, including whatever small item helps them to be more comfortable. Cots and linens should be cleaned weekly.

3. Allow children to take books to their cots. After five minutes or so, have all books put under cots and turn out the lights.

4. Limit napping to one hour; longer periods tend to result in children having trouble falling asleep at bedtime.

5. Make a chart of who sleeps and who does not the first week of school; arrange the children around the room accordingly. Strategically place the non-sleepers in places where they do not disturb the sleepers. After a half-hour of resting, quiet alternative activities can be made available for non-sleepers.

6. Always place the child's cot or mat in the same place in the room.

7. Rub the backs of children to help them fall asleep; it can work wonders! Many children who never take naps will often fall asleep if their backs are rubbed. Back rubbing can be combined with verbal and physical reinforcement for those who are resting quietly. It really does calm down those who are fidgety and allows their bodies to relax. However, some children do not like their backs rubbed and the caregiver must respect the child's wishes. Some programs also have quiet music, adults singing, or taped stories during rest time.

At first, families may complain. A parent may say, "My child has not napped since he was two!" Make it clear that the children are not expected to sleep or forced to sleep. Rather this is an opportunity to rest quietly for 20 to 30 minutes, which is beneficial to all children. Children who complain at first get used to the rest time and may grow to enjoy it. Many children who never used to nap will actually fall asleep. Rest time is an opportunity to help children learn how to pace themselves.

Age Grouping

School-age children's needs, wants and development are quite different from those of preschool children. While kindergarten-age children still enjoy activities similar to preschoolers' interests, the older children will have nothing to do with "baby stuff." Many caregivers make the mistake of treating children as if they were all the same age. With a range of children from kindergarten to sixth grade and sometimes older, children must be treated according to their developmental and individual needs. Nevertheless, mixed-age grouping does prove enjoyable for the children. The older children can serve as helpers, friends and role models for the younger ones. However, there should be time when children are age-grouped for specific activities such as certain games, special art activities, science, and other learning or problem solving projects. Vary schedules so that during some times, the children are age-grouped, and at other times, they can mix freely.

The Older Children

One of the most challenging areas in school-age care is working with the older children. In some programs, fourth through sixth graders are considered "the older children;" in others it is the third through fifth graders. This will vary, depending on the ages served and group sizes. Many older children have been in care since early childhood and would rather be home on their own. We, as professionals, know that it is safer for them to remain in programs, but for the children it can be very frustrating. The needs of the older children are quite different from the younger children. Challenge the older children with activities that meet their interests and developmental levels.

The Voice of Experience

At one time in our program, the third grade had a corner of the large room that was just for them with their own games and books. They often put up signs that stated, "Third graders, teachers and parents or guardians only. All other children KEEP OUT!"

The fourth and fifth grades use the school library after school and set it up as a recreational area. They have their own games, hobbies and crafts, equipment, radio and rules. They are free to join the younger children during free-play time but the younger children cannot come into their space. This arrangement works well with the children in our program.

57

10 hints for a successful program for older children

1. Provide a space or area just for them. Separate rooms are the best solution. If this is not possible, try setting up a corner of the room for them. Make this area off-limits for any younger child. Include in this area: age-appropriate games, a rug, a sofa, and bean-bag chairs or futons, a tape recorder/radio, art supplies, models, etc. In addition, equipment such as a Caroom™ board, ping-pong table, air hockey and a pool table are appropriate. Nerf™ pool or ping-pong sets are great.

2. Many older children have had years of painting and process-oriented art projects. Older children are not as process oriented as younger ones and are ready for kits, models and other challenging projects. They are interested in activities that have a goal and are ready to learn techniques and work on long-term projects. They also enjoy the occasional hands-on messy project.

3. Invite the older children to be helpers for the younger children. They can assist during homework time, art time, group or snack time. The older children may want to "adopt" a younger child and be their special helper. This has been very successful in our program.

4. Allow space away from adults for the older children. Supervise them, but try to keep a proper distance; do not intrude on their personal conversations and space unless it is necessary for safety.

5. Social problem solving and group dynamics are very important for the older group of children. Teachers need to help build a sense of group acceptance and togetherness.

6. Older children must learn to take responsibility for themselves and their actions. They can help establish their own rules and consequences.

7. Older children especially need ample time to exercise and be outside.

8. Outdoor games should be of their own choosing. Much socializing and modeling goes on at these times. Rules are an important part of the process. Adults should interfere only if rules are unfair or exclude some children.

9. Older children often invent their own games and play them for long periods. Encourage this process; it is important for their growth and development.

10. Older children should have a stronger voice in the program planning and implementation.

The Voice of Experience

We offer middle-school programs for youth who leave our program to attend middle school. Therefore, it is very important that we keep a large group of fifth graders. The techniques mentioned here have allowed us to be successful in retaining older children.

Beginning hormonal development will result in a newfound interest in the opposite sex. Children are maturing very early these days and the older group of children may act like adolescents from time to time. There will be sexual talk, embarrassment, modeling of older siblings, and exploration.

Children need to learn the sexual facts correctly. Often the children who are verbal about sex can be the ones who know the least about the subject. If a group leader plans to discuss sex with the older group of children, each child's parent should sign a parental permission slip. This is a legal consideration, especially for programs functioning within the public school system. A parent meeting at orientation/enrollment time might be useful and pave the way for uneasy parents or guardians. Unfortunately, a child whose parent will not agree to allow them to participate will need to be gently excluded. Remember that although the teacher may not talk to a particular child, the other children will relay the information.

Discussions about sex are best when they occur naturally, spontaneously or at the children's request. Keep the discussions honest, simple and straightforward. If the teacher does not have an answer, he or she should say so and then look it up. There are many good books about this subject.

If you strive to meet the needs of the older group of children, then their time in child care can be more enjoyable for everyone. With a space of their own, the older children will feel they are special and have earned the right to more freedom than the younger ones. The younger children see that they have something to look forward to in your program when they are older.

Middle-School Programs

The middle-school years are characterized by growth and change. Young adolescents are rapidly changing physically, emotionally and socially. This is a time to explore, establish new values, develop talents and life-long interests. Youth may experiment with drugs and alcohol and become sexually active during these years. SAC programs for this age group must provide positive role models, physical activities, opportunities to expand views, and intellectual stimulation. These aspects of a middle-school program help youth adjust to their growing minds and bodies.

If a SAC program is doing a good job of meeting the needs of older elementary children, parents may request care during the middle-school years.

The Voice of Experience   **Our Middle-School Program**

West Portal C.A.R.E., Inc. in San Francisco, in response to requests to continue care in middle school, opened *After-School Pursuits* (ASP) in 1992. The program is housed at a large middle school and uses shared space in the school cafeteria. ASP began with six to ten youth per day and now serves over 75 daily. In San Mateo County, California, Ralston After-Middle School (RAMS), serving 50 youth, and Club Central operate through Cipriani After-School. Both programs are housed in large rooms separated into interest areas. The environments include recreational game tables, several computers, TVs with game systems and movies, a snack and cooking area, several tables for homework, and a large sofa area with plenty of age-appropriate books and magazines. There are materials for arts and crafts, including soap and candle making, jewelry making, masks and ceramics. Snack is set up for self-service when the youth arrive, with plenty from which to choose. Youth help prepare and clean up this nutritious snack. *Friday Night Out* (FNO) occurs once a month and is an outing into the community from 5:30 to 8:30 PM. Favorite trips include the movies, laser tag, the mall, ice skating, rock climbing, bowling and live performances. The youth pay for dinner and the program subsidizes the field trip. *Friday Night In* (FNI) occurs once a month. The center is open until 8:30 PM for recreational fun and dinner. Youth and their families enjoy both the FNO and FNI events.

Middle-School Program Tips

- Call the program something inventive and creative, attractive to middle-school youth.

- Staff must be trained in youth development needs.

- Staff must be considered good role models.

- Middle-school youth need a separate space from the younger children.

- Middle-school youth need to have a high degree of involvement in program planning.

- Enrollment must be flexible to accommodate growing independence and other out-of-school-time activities.

- Staff must keep in mind the nutritional needs of adolescents.

- Homework assistance must be a central component of the program, as academic levels increase. Staff must be competent to help with the academic needs.

- Recreational activities and a variety of choices should be included when time permits.

- Allowing time to socialize is essential.

- Foster team-building skills.

- Service learning projects allow the youth to give back to and support the community.

- If possible, offer Friday Night Outings (FNO) or a Friday Night In (FNI) program.

Summer Programs for Middle-School Youth

Summer camp programs, especially for middle-school youth, are well received in most communities. Whereas several options for elementary-school children are available in the summer, there are fewer programs available for middle-school youth.

The Voice of Experience

After-School Pursuits has been running a summer camp program for many years. I have also run a specialized summer camp called "Hands-On" Science and Adventure Camp, funded through the American Business Collaboration for Quality Dependent Care for three summers. This camp included an on-site ropes challenge course integrated with a "hands-on" science curriculum.

9 strategies for planning a summer camp program for middle-school youth

1. Speak to the youth and ask them what activities are interesting. Include youth when planning camp, as youth "buy-in" will make a successful camp.

2. Develop a flexible program for youth. For youth attending academic summer school, provide a before-and-after-summer school program. Camp sessions should be one or two weeks in length because youth want to choose a variety of activities in the summer.

3. Provide as many opportunities as your budget and transportation system can support. Use the camp location as a home base and then use what is available in your community to help the youth explore the world around them. Field trips to amusement parks, water parks, overnight camping trips, professional sports games, laser tag, video arcades, museums, recreational areas, beaches, pools and local colleges are popular.

4. Encourage physical activity. Help youth explore a variety of physical games and sports. Sports outings such as rowing on a lake, indoor rock climbing, ice-skating, roller-skating, skateboarding, bike riding, fencing, and a visit to a pool hall can be built into the program on a weekly basis along with field trips and local outings.

5. Teach life skills. Use a counselor-in-training model for interested youth. [*At RAMS*, youth volunteer as counselors-in-training, spending three hours per week working with younger children. They are supervised, receive training and have an opportunity to ask questions and problem solve about their experience working with children. They sign a contract, work with center staff and are evaluated.*]

6. Allow the youth to create businesses to raise money. The money can be used to offset the cost of field trips that are more expensive or as a donation to an organization of the youth's choice. Youth are responsible for the planning, implementing and evaluating of the endeavor. This is a good opportunity to learn about setting and achieving goals, accounting and retailing, and social skills. [*At RAMS*, the program is called Young Entrepreneurs. Youth plan several fund-raising activities throughout the summer, such as a hot dog lunch for the other camps or an arts and crafts sale*].

7. Specialty camps are great for this group. Camps that focus on science, sports, visual or performing arts, computers, outdoor skills or music are big draws. If you plan to offer a specialty camp, keep room in your schedule for some traditional camp activities to balance the camp experience.

8. Involve the families. Offer family nights for youth to highlight what they are doing or have learned in camp. Family night can be a potluck dinner or youth can serve dinner to their family. You can even make it a fundraiser.

9. Youth and their families should evaluate the camp each summer. Use their comments to improve the program for the next summer.

Interest Clubs

An excellent way to involve children and staff is interest clubs. When interviewing potential staff candidates, ask what special interests or skills they possess that might make an interesting club. After a staff person is hired, he or she creates a list of activities, hobbies and areas of expertise he or she is interested in teaching to a small group of children. One hour per week, children meet in "KIDS' CLUBS." Each child signs up for a first, second and third choice of clubs and each child is put into one of their club choices. This encourages a variety of activities and social groupings. Children participate in a specific club for four weeks and then sign up for a new club.

Interest Club Ideas:

Basketball	Tumbling	Science	Wood working
Music	Rug hooking	Crocheting	Leather crafts
Sewing	Printing	Karaoke	Candle making
Tie dying	Silk screening	Papier-mâché	Ceramics
Radio show	Wrestling	Puppetry	Computers
Photography	Outdoor games	Mural painting	Mask making
Baseball	Soccer	Paper airplanes	Volleyball
Track	Mime	Photography	Gardening
Mechanics	Sign language	Practical jokes	Foreign language
Origami	Beading	Quilting	Cooking
Blender drinks	Drama	Dance	Soap making
Making board games	Comics	Newspaper publication	Movement/ Jazzercise

Ideas are limited only by staff interest and motivation. Clubs provide an excellent way for children to explore areas of interest in depth, to learn new skills, and to give the adults an opportunity to teach children something they enjoy. These clubs are mixed-aged groups, which allow older children to interact with and help younger ones, and vice versa. Interest clubs are wonderful for programs with 40 children or more, but also work with smaller programs. Interest clubs allow large programs to do expensive and more complicated projects with smaller groups of children.

One staff person should be designated as the "floater." The floater assists where needed. Community volunteers can serve as floaters or lead a club if they have a talent they want to share. Clubs needing

more supervision, such as candle making, cooking and wood working, have smaller enrollment or have an additional adult present to assist.

Interest clubs have proven to be a very successful feature of our program. Children look forward to these weekly classes, and parents enjoy the new skills children are learning. Staff enjoy sharing interests and creativity with children and youth.

Summer Programs and Holiday Care

The scheduling for all-day programs is quite different from before-and-after-school only. Long blocks of time allow more variety of activities, field trips and ongoing projects. For all-day care, such as holidays or teacher in-service days, provide at least two snacks per day in addition to lunch. Other activities include free choice time, much outdoor play and recreation, interesting field trips, and (in the summer) lessons such as karate, swimming and dance. A quiet rest time should be built into the schedule for all children. This can include reading and being read to, doing puzzles, and other quiet activities.

Themes work well for all-day and summer programs. However, many of the children have been in child care since they were very small and have done the standard preschool themes. Try to make the school-age themes as new and engaging as possible. Activities such as snack, dramatic play, art, cooking, field trips, and science can all center on the themes. You may want to plan an overall theme such as WOW Camp (World Of Water) with sub themes every week or two weeks or a different theme each week.

In summer and holiday programs, emphasize the differences in the program from the school year. When naming a summer session, use a name similar to a summer camp or day camp. This will help change the emphasis and children's attitude. In full-day programs, emphasize a relaxed, fun atmosphere rather than academics.

To add excitement to your summer program, schedule in a special event. This can be a game, party, visit from someone to the program, performance by the children, or a contest. In our summer program, we have one special event every one to two weeks. The events can be theme related or not. *(See page 66 for summer theme and special event ideas.)*

The Voice of Experience **Our summer program schedule:**

7:00-9:00	Free choice
9:00-9:15	Morning group
9:15-10:30	Morning activity time (crafts, science, nature, sports)
10:30-10:45	Snack (A.M. snack should be light)
10:45-11:45	Activity time (theme-related activities, special events, clubs, swimming lessons, water play, etc.)
11:45-12:30	Clean up and lunch
12:30-1:00	Outdoor play
1:00-1:15	Group time (kindergartners calm down for rest)
1:15-1:45	Resting and quiet activity time (rest from 1:15-2:30)
1:45-3:30	Activity time (theme-related activities, cooking, woodworking, lessons, etc.)
3:30-3:45	Snack time
3:45-4:00	Afternoon group (Can be broken into small groups)
4:00-6:00	Free choice/free play indoors/outdoors

(One day each week includes a full day field trip.)

Summer Theme Ideas:

Ecology	Animals	Under the Sea	Bays
Olympics	Space and Stars	Hooray for Hollywood	Jungles
Into the Past	Toys	Sports	Myth and Fantasy
Deserts	Endangered Species	International Foods	Fads
Pets	Collections	Weather	Geography
Dinosaurs	Super Heroes	Prehistoric Times	The Gold Rush
Disneyland ™	Reptiles	Nature	Aeronautics
History	Magic	Electronics	Water Sports
Safari	Mad Scientist	Environmental Studies	Explorers
Gizmos and Gadgets	Make a Movie	World Travel	Fashion
Communication	The Seashore	Around the World	Back to the Future
Inventions	Archaeology	Let's Put On A Show	Color

Ideas for special events:

Carnival	Un-birthday Party	Lost Treasure Day	Sand Castle Contest
Puppet Show	Restaurant Day	Kite/airplane contest	Backwards Day
Winter in the Summer	Olympics	Relay Races	Office Day
Outer Space Day	Mystery Day	Square Dancing	Build a Volcano
Soap Bubble Contest	Cartoon Dress-up Day	Line Dancing	Water Mania
Sock Hop	Chinese Cooking	Mexican Cooking	Car Wash
Pet Wash	Crafts Sale	BBQ	Old Fashioned Picnic
Teddy Bear Picnic	Trading Cards Day	Lip syncing contest	Luau
Wild West Day	Crazy Hair Day	PJ Party	Secret Pals
Scavenger Hunt	Talent Show	Detective Day	
Crafts Day	Cook-Off	Mad Scientist Inventions	

One method that works well in summer programs is for each group leader to plan one project a week in a particular interest area. Connect the projects with the themes. Divide the children into age groups (as evenly as possible). Allow each age group a chance to do each teacher's project on a particular day and at a specific time. There are many ways to organize projects for small and larger groups. Test what works best with your staff and children.

For programs that are in a very hot climate, outside time is best in the morning and lots of water play will help beat the heat. For cold weather scheduling, take advantage of the sun. Remember to be flexible with scheduling. Circumstances change and there are no strict periods.

Field Trips and Special Programs

Field trips are a very important, enriching, and integral part of school-age programs. Riding public transportation is a new experience for many children and can be very educational. In addition, many children do not have opportunities to explore their cities, towns and environments.

Some areas do not have good public transportation available. If it is too difficult to manage many field trips, then in-house field trips or special events can be substituted or used to enrich program themes. Many museums have staff who will come to the program. For information and vehicle tours, invite public service people such as police, fire and paramedics to visit your center. The local animal shelter worker, park or forest ranger, zoo staff or veterinarian may bring in animals. Arrange for a mime troop, a clown, folk singers or a storyteller to come and perform. Parents, business people, and others such as grandparents, aunts, uncles, friends and neighbors may also volunteer to talk about their professions. Also, invite hobbyists, retired persons that have special interests, farmers, professional athletes and professional organizations to speak. These people help to diversify the children's experiences and give them something out of the ordinary to look forward to while in full-day programs.

11 hints for successful field trips

1. When selecting a field trip have a staff member visit the site in advance.

2. Make reservations for the field trip in advance and pay fees.

3. It is a good idea to call the place the day before to reconfirm.

4. Be well staffed; include parent volunteers if possible.

5. Each teacher of a group of children should bring along a small first-aid kit, emergency releases, tissues and/or wet wipes.

6. Dress the children in a school T-shirt (in bright colors easy to see in a crowd), or other identifying article of clothing such as a scarf or a baseball cap. Each child should bring a jacket or sweater. (*In our program, the children wear tie-dyed shirts and carry camp backpacks.*)

7. Have children bring lunches in paper bags stowed inside their backpacks (no glass containers).

8. Make sure the children know the field trip rules ahead of time, are aware of where and why they are going, and what mode of transportation is being used. Also, make sure they know what to do if they get lost from the group.

9. When walking in small groups (4-10), the adult should walk in the middle of the group (if there is only one adult). For larger groups or situations where there are two or more adults, have one adult lead the group, one adult in the middle and one adult at the end of the line.

10. Children should never cross the street alone and should stay within the crosswalks. For crowded intersections, have one adult stand in the middle of the street to stop traffic if necessary.

11. Encourage the children to write thank you notes when appropriate.

One of the most exciting opportunities presented by a summer program is taking longer field trips to further destinations. Even though this is a great expense, a field trip out of your local area can be exciting, fun and very rewarding. It can also present some challenges.

Tips for riding on buses:

- Make sure children know the bus rules.

- Everyone goes to the bathroom before leaving.

- Know the names of the children and staff on the bus. Keep an accurate count.

- Plan activities for bus rides: singing is a great bus activity; appoint a song leader for each bus.

- Have staff situated throughout the bus, sitting strategically.

- Bring a box with things for long rides – lanyard, string, playing cards, crafts, etc.

- Have a first aid kit and bus sick-kid box.

- Count children regularly.

- If possible, include a staff person driving a car.

- Have directions, maps, emergency telephone numbers, cell phone.

- Identify a staff person as sweeper - the last off the bus.

- Identify a staff bus leader – this person talks to the driver, counts the children, and communicates with other buses or the site.

- For late afternoon returns – make it quiet time, rest time.

- Make sure the bus company and driver are well aware of your schedule.

Walking trips to parks, historical or local sites and trails can be valuable when transportation is not possible. There are several things to remember for walking trips:

- Make sure the distance is manageable for the age group.

- Find a place to rest along the way before starting out.

- Carry water and paper cups and an easy snack for energy.

- Always have at least two adults present.

- Prepare ahead for weather, especially during fall and spring.

- Advise children and staff to wear walking shoes.

Using parents' cars for field trips raises questions about insurance liabilities. Ask your insurance agent to research the best method for making field trips possible. Try asking the local Rotary Club, Elks Club or other organizations to donate a van and keep it serviced. Do what you can to get out and into the community.

Field trip suggestions:
(Look for what is interesting and accessible in your area)

museums of all kinds	the zoo	parks	botanical gardens
bowling	hospitals	boat rides	movies
neighborhood walks	picnics	bakery	restaurant tours
baseball games	swimming pools	water slides	amusement parks
lakes or ponds	pet shops	fishing	TV or radio stations
ice skating	roller skating	live theater	the circus
the mountains	a puppet show	the beach	a farm
factory/plant tours	magic show	horseback riding	the airport
the country	the arboretum	wildlife preserves	a train ride
miniature golf	recreation centers	ferry boat rides	camp-outs
indoor rock climbing			

Projects

The focus in most public schools for many years has been academic success for all. One aspect of working with children in an out-of-school setting is supporting and enhancing the classroom experience as a complement to the school day. Care providers should visit the children's classrooms to observe what is being emphasized and be aware of state and district content standards for the grade levels they serve. Communication with classroom teachers can help staff to broaden, enrich and supplement the academic day.

Due to curriculum requirements some schools offer very little hands-on exposure to the visual and performing arts, problem solving and science. For many teachers, art means a specific lesson or preconceived purpose; the results come out looking the same. Art projects in elementary schools tend to be product oriented rather than process oriented. Few teachers, in grades higher than kindergarten, put out an easel and encourage free expression or allow the children to "mess around" with paint. An easel is a great gift to some children. Hands-on and experimental science projects are often missing from many school curricula. The projects in this book were chosen with these factors in mind.

Open-Ended Projects

In an open-ended project, the emphasis is on the process the child goes through in creating. An open-ended project means that there is no expected outcome. A finished product will vary depending on the child and the materials.

The process of using the materials and exploring the possibilities of each medium is the focus of open-ended activities. There are no wrong or right ways to create them. Open-ended projects reflect the individual child's personality and perspective and thus offer an alternative to having twenty items that come out looking the same. In a closed-ended or product-oriented project, the outcome is the most important result. These projects are known as "parent pleasers." They have certain expected outcomes and teachers help the children achieve these goals. Individuality and creativity aside, children's small motor skills are often not well developed and it is frustrating for them to be asked to try to copy a teacher-made model, especially if it is an intricate or detailed activity.

Having an area where children can choose projects for themselves gives them a chance to explore and develop their creative skills. Support and encourage children but never do the project for them. They have an endless ability to create new and imaginative things out of any given material. Allow children to stretch and challenge their skills through their own creativity. Open-ended projects can include drama, arts & crafts and science and nature exploration.

Kits and Finished Products

As children grow, mature, and have many experiences creating open-ended projects, they become ready for kits and finished products. Usually children in third grade and older enjoy doing kits such as basket weaving, string art, leather crafts, or beading. A balance between kits and open-ended art projects is advisable. The process is still the most valuable aspect, but the product begins to take on its own importance. Finished products in science are exciting, but the process of inquiry should be the prime focus. Allow time and offer opportunities to use the material more than one way.

Planning And Project Set-Up

During the planning process of a particular project, there are many components to keep in mind. The most important are the ages, interests and abilities of the children. Projects should be planned ahead so any special materials can be collected or purchased. Science projects and experiments with a specific goal should be tested in advance to insure that the teacher knows what to expect. Make children a part of the planning process. Ask them what projects interest and excite them and let them know that their ideas and suggestions are important. When planning a project it is critical to allocate enough time for children to explore the medium or tools before working toward a finished product. All creative approaches are acceptable.

Set-up is critical when presenting a project. Children can help set up the materials. Children enjoy mixing paints, putting newspaper on the art table, making dough or clay and cutting out materials for projects. Make sure that all the materials are available and in large enough quantities for the majority of children doing the activity. If the project is messy, covering the table with newspaper, butcher paper or plastic will prevent a long cleanup. If the materials are presented in an attractive way, the children will be more likely to try the project. Make sure there is plenty of room for all the materials needed or set some aside for later use.

Give each child his or her own materials, provide easy access to shared materials or have children rotate through the project in small groups. If a table cannot accommodate all the children choosing to do the project, start a waiting list and have the children call each other when a space becomes available. When doing a project, observe what works well and what does not and use this information for future planning. Flexibility is also very important.

Include children in the clean-up process. This provides an opportunity for learning cooperation and taking on a sense of ownership in the program.

Examples

Examples are not usually necessary. Many teachers do not want a preconceived product, but rather desire children to be able to create their own outcome to particular projects. However, there are times when a planned project is set on the art table; without an example, it would be very difficult for the children to envision what they can achieve with the materials. In these cases, after showing an example put it out of sight to allow individual variation and creativity. Examples should always look like a child has created them and several diverse examples are even better. When the examples look like they were created by an adult, children may feel frustrated that their work is "not as good" as the adult. Save pieces of children's work to use as examples for the future. After the project is completed, evaluate whether the model was necessary for future presentation.

Projects and Activities With Food

There are art activities and projects in this book that include the use of food. This is admittedly a controversial practice because there is so much hunger in the world. For many children items like rice and beans are staples of their daily diet. It is difficult for them to understand why this food is being used in a non-nutritive fashion. Be sensitive to this problem. We have included these projects because although they are controversial, they still have educational and hands-on value. We provide a variety of other activities, including alternatives to the use of food. Develop your own philosophy regarding the use of food and use discretion.

Unsuccessful Projects

It is important for child care workers to understand that not every project is going to be a success. What works well with one group of children can be a disaster with another. The most carefully planned project may not work out as anticipated. If a project is not successful for one reason or another, it is not the end of the world. The most experienced teacher has had projects fail. The teacher can evaluate

the project to try to determine the cause of the "failure" and learn from the mistakes. In many cases, the adult leader will discover that the failure was due to factors not under the adult's control.

The children are not to blame for an unsuccessful project. It is our professional responsibility to support the children when projects are not successful. They need reassurance that the goof-up was not their fault and that their feelings of frustration and anger are acceptable. When the failure is due to something that can be altered in the set-up or the process, make a note of it and try again. Experiment with changing some of the materials or tools, the procedure, timing, location, or the age group of the children. During a project, it is sometimes easy to spot what is going wrong. Do not hesitate to correct it right away. Change or stop what you are doing when it becomes necessary. Science projects often go awry due to timing, the group composition or unfamiliarity with either the process or the materials. Trying out a project ahead of time will help prevent (but not necessarily eliminate) the failure syndrome when a specific result is desired. Other times, as long as a teacher is familiar with the use of materials, there is no failure possible. Remember that the process of exploring provides its own success, no matter what the consequences.

The Activities

Rough & Tumble Play

Problem-Solving Activities

Science Activities

Three-Dimensional Art

Wax & Crayons

Candle Making

Planting & Growing

Crafts Recipes

Gifts

Puppetry

Masks

Nature Crafts

Indoor & Outdoor Games

Conflict Resolution Activities

Conflict resolution activities involve building the respect and dignity of each person in the group. Group activities that foster sharing, communication, and support are a vital part of the role of the after-school situation. Children need to feel that they are important and that their ideas and opinions have value. They also need to develop awareness of the ideas and experiences of others. The *Tribes** training system or *Adventures in Peacemaking** offer methods for presenting group sharing games; both are excellent sources for ideas and activities that introduce people to each other and allow them to learn, share, and accept differences. These methods can be very helpful in combating the pressure of peer conformity and the clique tendencies of older children. These concepts and games can also be extended into other areas of family life and after-school programs.

There are other books listed in the *Resource Section* that have group communication games that enhance children's ability to decide and speak for themselves, while still acknowledging the individuality of their friends.

If your program is associated with a school that is using a specific conflict resolution curriculum or methodology, consider adopting it for your program. The consistency and continuity will be invaluable for the children.

Social Problem Solving Activities

In all activities of this nature, there are several rules that need to be taught and adhered to by everyone, including the teacher.

- The right to pass — anyone may choose not to talk.

- No put downs — any idea is worth discussion.

- Good listening — courtesy and attention when another talks.

- Confidentiality — what is said is not discussed out of group.

---

*Gibbs, Jeanne. *Tribes*. Sausalito: CenterSource Systems. 1995.

*Kreidler, William and Lisa Furlong. *Adventures in Peacemaking*. Cambridge: Educators for Social Responsibility. 1995.

Thumbs Up/Down   For Grades K - 6

Purpose: This game helps children to develop decision-making skills, express their opinions visibly and be aware of different opinions. It can help focus on the strength of peer pressure.

Materials: A list of age-appropriate questions or statements. (Teacher makes these up. Example: Hot dogs taste better than hamburgers.)

Procedure:

1. Sit the whole group in a circle on chairs.

2. Explain the rules:

> a. The teacher will make a statement, the children will indicate if they agree with it or not.
>
> b. If they strongly agree, they are to clap and cheer loudly.
>
> c. If they agree, they are to raise thumbs up.
>
> d. If they disagree, they give thumbs down.
>
> e. If they strongly disagree, they are to boo, hiss, and stamp.
>
> f. If they have no opinion, they are to fold their arms and say nothing at all.

3. When you have asked all questions, it is time to discuss the process:

> a. Was it hard to do? Allow each child to talk by going around the circle quickly.
>
> b. Did their friends vote differently?
>
> c. Did they find themselves changing their votes?
>
> d. What did they feel while doing this game?

4. Go around the circle again and have every child state something that the child liked or did not like about the game.

Comments: This game lets children see how easily a group sways them. It works as a great confidence builder especially for children who are reluctant to vocalize their opinions due to peer pressure. Make sure the questions are non-threatening, and not likely to change any current rules in the program.

I Like My Neighbor   For Grades K - 6

Purpose: To include every child, promote awareness of similarities and differences.

Materials: Enough chairs or carpet squares for each child.

Procedure:

1. Sit children in circle on chairs facing inward.

2. The teacher starts, so there is one chair too few.

3. Explain the rules:

   a. The person with no chair will say, I like my neighbors, especially those with _____ (brown hair, tennis shoes, etc.).

   b. When the person in the middle says something that the children have, they are to get up quickly and move to another chair.

   c. The children must get up, may not sit in their own chair again and may not stay in the middle.

   d. One person is left with no chair again. It is their turn to call something out.

   e. There is no pushing, running, sliding, or sitting on another child.

Comments: This is a very noisy and active game. It allows all of the children to feel like part of the group.

Spider Web   For Grades: K - 6

Purpose: Developing verbal, sharing, and listening skills.

Materials: Large ball of yarn.

Procedure:

1. Seat group in a circle.

2. Ask any one question appropriate for your group, i.e. what is your favorite thing about autumn? What was the best, or worse, thing that happened to you this weekend?

3. Teacher starts. Hold the yarn ball and give your answer. Wrap the end of the yarn around your fingers or wrist and toss the ball across the circle from you. Name the person to whom you are tossing.

4. The person who gets the ball answers the question, wraps the yarn around their wrist or hand and tosses it across again to the person of their choice.

5. This process continues until everyone in the group has had a turn to talk and has the yarn wrapped. The last person should throw the yarn ball back to the teacher who started it, completing the web.

6. Look at the web of communication you have made and discuss it. Talk about how it would be different if it were done again. Look under it, over it, and even through it.

7. Putting it away can be done two ways:

     a. Lay the web down and dismiss the children, you roll it up.

     b. If you have time, reverse the procedure, and see if they can remember what the person who threw the ball to them said.

Graffitti   For Grades: 2 - 6

Purpose: To encourage sharing feelings and provide exposure to the wide range of values in any given group.

Materials: A large sheet of paper for each group, large marking pens.
Procedure:

1. Divide children into groups of four.

2. Give each group one piece of large paper with one of the following headings:

    Pet Peeves

    Favorite Moments

    Things That Scare Me

    Things That Make Me Happy

    Things That Make Me Curious

3. Each team will spend 3 minutes on the first paper. They may write any way they want, wherever they choose. After 3 minutes, they must stop writing. Pass each paper to a different group. Allow 3 minutes again. Repeat this process until every team has had each of the papers.

4. Step 4 can be done either of two ways, depending on the size of your whole group. Either: 1. Give each team one sheet and allow them 10 minutes to discuss trends. Then each team will present what they found to the whole group. Or: 2. Put the graffiti papers up and have the whole group spend a few minutes looking at them, then spend 10 minutes discussing what they see, i.e. similarities, differences, and other comparisons between group answers.

Comments: This activity promotes a lot of comments and laughter. Be prepared for some unusual and diverse graffiti to discuss.

Rough & Tumble Play

Teachers in out-of-school programs are primarily female, and often sensitive and caring people. Because of this, they are usually very quick to spot rough play and to redirect it to a more focused or quieter activity. There is research and experimentation available which questions the value of halting all rough play. Most, though by no means all, of the children engaging in roughhousing type of play are boys. They jump on each other, wrestle, play hit, push, chase, yell and generally raise the energy level in any schoolyard or room. While this may not be conducive to a calm program, it probably should be encouraged in a structured way that allows room and time for the children to channel this energy in safe ways, to help children learn ways to manage impulse control, learn how to appropriately use their bodies and have fun.

There are obvious differences between the body language of those children who are engaged in play fighting and those who are seriously angry. A seriously angry child may have closed fists, an angry expression on his or her face and may use unacceptable language. Whereas children participating in rough and tumble play tend to laugh, have open fists, have friendly facial expressions and use bantering words. Pellegrini and Perlmutter found in their research article in the January 1988 issue of *Young Children* that boys who engaged successfully in rough and tumble had better developed social skills and were more liked by their peers in general. They found that those who did not function well in play fight situations, or in games with rules and strategies, more often could not relate to their peers without becoming angry, were less socially skilled, and less liked. This research could be an important beginning to finding ways to help children with poor social coping skills. Rough and tumble play can teach them to relate better with peers and enjoy playground activities more. The skills they learn in normal, supervised, rough and tumble activities can be applied to other types of social situations.

While there are no firm conclusions yet, the research shows that roughhousing is a very normal way for many children to relate to each other. Fathers may play with their children generally with more toss and bounce than do mothers. It is a form of demonstrating affection and love. Children whose parents show affection in these ways learn that it is safe to tell a friend you like them by pushing, jumping on and wrestling with them. Instead of negating their spontaneous show of friendship, it would be healthier to allow them to express that energy and affection in organized activities.

Girls will benefit from this type of activity also. Many girls have few opportunities to learn the rules of team sports, to assert themselves, or to engage in assertive play. These girls are often timid first, but establish their courage with practice. While they develop a new type of self-confidence, they are also developing a new awareness of themselves. They look forward to the wrestling time and begin to want to go against the boys. For aggressive girls, this controlled environment is an acceptable outlet for otherwise discouraged behavior. The girls in our program are some of the most interested participants when we wrestle.

10 suggestions for safe roughhousing

1. Set a time limit for the whole activity – half an hour is good.

2. Define the space.

3. Use mats, carpets, or other soft surfaces.

4. Have children remove shoes and belts, and other accessories.

5. Supervise adequately – two teachers are best.

6. If there is an injury, stop, attend to the child, then continue. Injuries are usually heads and egos.

7. Remind children that this is for fun only, not to hurt, get even, or compete.

8. Watch body language. If a child gets upset, have him/her stop and wait until he/she is calm again.

9. Children not following directions must leave the area for the rest of the activity time. **Important: Give only one warning.**

10. No pulling clothes, biting, kicking, pinching, choking, punching or other injurious action. With attention to these rules, this type of activity will NOT degenerate into fighting.

Wrestling For Grades: K-6

Materials: A large mat or two small ones and enough space for the safety of the onlookers, a watch with a second hand, a whistle (optional).

Procedure:

1. Explain the rules.

    a. Wrestle only with an adult at the mat.

    b. Open fists at all times.

    c. No kicking, biting, hair pulling, pinching, chokeholds or headlocks, high body slams, or karate chops. (Use your judgment)

    d. Wrestlers must stay on the mat. Spectators must stay off.

    e. No activity starts until the whistle blows or a signal is given and it stops immediately when it repeats.

    f. Matches last 60-120 seconds depending on the age of the children.

    g. If a child gets upset or injured, he/she should say so.

    h. Matches need to be even in terms of size at first. Girls will not necessarily always wrestle other girls.

2. Spectators sit on the sidelines AND MUST STAY THERE. Spectators who wrestle out of turn are removed from the area entirely. Cheering is for both participants.

3. The teacher approves and times the matches. Later children can choose younger wrestling partners.

4. The whistle is a valuable assistant in this activity.

5. Pre-arrange verbal signals with the children so that a participant can halt the match by using the signal if they need to stop.

Comments: Variation: place a wide line of tape down the center of the mat. Contestants stand facing each other on the line. When the whistle blows, they try to push each other off the line of tape entirely. A foot or hand still on the line counts and the play continues until one of them has no more contact with the tape.

Ball Throw   For Grades: K-6

Materials: A box of spongy or foam balls, and a whistle. Use three balls for every two children. Do this in a large indoor space to allow running.

Procedure:

1. Seat children in a big circle. Tell them that when the whistle sounds they are going to throw balls at each other (and at you) until the whistle signals "Stop".

2. Dump the balls into the middle of the circle, get out of the way and blow the whistle. Grab a couple balls and throw them.

3. Allow 15 minutes or so, and then blow the whistle to stop.

4. Everyone helps to return the balls to the box.

Comments: There is a good feeling on everyone's part, and a lot of energy expended. For a variation, place a piece of tape down the center of the room dividing it evenly. Form two teams. The team with the fewest number of balls on their side of the tape at the end wins.

Bopping   For Grades: K-6

Materials: Two socks each with a foam ball in it, or a commercial bopper set, a stopwatch, and a whistle.

Procedure:

1. Sit children in a circle around mat or defined space.

2. Explain that they are going to "bop" each other for 1-2 minutes.

3. No head or face shots are allowed, nor is hitting around genital areas.

4. Select a match and let them go.

5. Blow the whistle to stop.

Paper Wars   For Grades: K-6

Materials: A large pile of paper that you do not need (secondhand computer paper is the best), and a large indoor space.

Procedure:

1. Each child takes a handful of the paper and crumbles it up to make balls. Each child has his or her own pile.

2. While they are doing that, the teacher puts a piece of tape dividing the space in half.

3. Split the children into two groups and sit them in their "base" on either side of the room.

4. The children stand and aim for the other side when the whistle blows. They may not cross the line.

5. If they are hit, they are out and sit on the sidelines.

6. The last two still throwing balls, are "galaxy rulers" (or whatever you choose to call them).

Comments: This will create a big mess and a lot of fun. You can allow the game to be played without children getting "out." Tell them that when the whistle blows twice they are to go steal someone else's supply of balls and the "winner" is the person with the most balls in their corner. Alternatively, play it with no winners at all.

Balloon Stomp   For Grades: 2-6

Materials: Two balloons per child, a large indoor space (or outdoors if enclosed and not windy).

Procedure:

1. Blow up balloons before hand, or have older children help.

2. Seat children along the sidelines of the space.

3. Turn the balloons loose.

4. Turn the children loose.

5. The idea is to step on and pop all the balloons. This is a free-for-all.

6. Make sure you tell them, NO HANDS.

Comments: This game provides a very fun and NOISY time for all! Another way to play is to divide children into teams, and have balloons that are two different colors. They try to stomp on the other team's balloons.

A second variation is to tie the balloons onto children's ankles with yarn or other soft string. They are to stomp on other players balloons, while protecting their own.

Pile On   For Grades: K-6

Materials: Pillows, cushions (a rug area preferably) and a whistle.

Procedure:

1. This is an all time favorite of children between kindergarten and second grade.

2. Seat children around the rug edges.

3. Place the pillows in the middle of the area.

4. Explain the rules: no hitting, pinching, biting, head bumping; only piling on.

5. Select 4-8 children for each round (use your discretion about which children will work, and which ones are better off waiting until the next pile).

6. Blow the whistle. Let them pile onto each other on top of the pillows for 1-2 minutes. How high can it get without the top person sliding off? Keep your eyes on the bottom person(s); they have the right to call "Stop" before the timer.

Comments: There may be a bumped head or two, but mostly a lot of friendly jostling and laughter. The children may imitate this activity on their own when you do not particularly want them to, so make sure the rule is clear that this activity may only take place with proper supervision and timing. Children who ignore the rules should be excluded the next time the activity is done. It will usually only take one such exclusion to set the rule firmly.

Problem Solving

Problem solving is the process which teaches children how to find answers to situations when the means to the solution is not necessarily obvious. It is "What to do when you don't know what to do." Teaching problem solving involves teaching children strategies for figuring out different ways to reach a conclusion.

Problem solving is a very important part of learning for children, and has recently been considered a major component to be developed and utilized in the California state school curriculum. Problem solving can be used in conjunction with all subjects including math, reading, language arts, social studies, arts and social skill development. Many problem solving games and activities take only a few minutes to plan and execute, and are usually fun as well as challenging children to problem solve.

It is important in teaching problem solving to state the technique you want children to learn during the game or activity, but not before they have had time to find it for themselves. The keys to problem solving, whatever the subject, are time and patience. You are teaching a thinking process; that means that some children will pick it up very quickly, and others will need repeated activities and more exposure to the process. It is essential that these games be fun for the children and do not appear to be work or "lessons."

Problem solving skills are a part of daily life for all adults. It is important that children have access to the techniques that will make it possible for them to function as completely as possible in all areas of their interests and needs. Many schools and teachers do not yet use problem-solving concepts in their teaching process. This is a valuable area for after-school providers to explore and expand. It can be exciting to see the interest and enthusiasm generated by these activities, and to watch the growth of skills and techniques in children.

Steps in Problem Solving

1. Gather information (in game situations teacher provides this.)

2. State the problem clearly. Define it.

3. Generate ideas to solve the problem.

4. Evaluate the answers and the process.

10 problem-solving strategies to teach children

This is a list of the strategies used to solve problems. Children should be taught these methods so they can rely on them. When one does not work, they need to be able to try another. This list is based on the California State Framework for Problem Solving. Each of these strategies can be applied to almost any problem area. They are all valuable to children and adults. See which ones are techniques that you use to solve your own problems.

1. Look for patterns.

2. Guess and check.

3. Write equations - (if...=....,then.....).

4. Use logical reasoning.

5. Work backwards.

6. Draw pictures of the problem or situation.

7. List information.

8. Make tables or graphs.

9. Act out or use hands-on equipment.

10. Simplify the problem by breaking it into smaller parts first.

Pico, Fermi, Bagels   For Grades: 2 - 6

Purpose: A problem solving game that teaches place value, and works something like the game Master Mind™.

Materials needed: Chalk and chalkboard, or large paper and marking pen placed on a wall for visibility.

Procedure:

1. Have children sit in groups in front of the writing surface.

2. Explain that you are going to play a game with them that involves two digit numbers (this can be expanded to three or four later). You are choosing a number that falls between 10-99, and writing it where they cannot see it. They have to guess what it is in the fewest number of guesses possible.

3. As they guess a number, you write it on the grid on the number side and then give them their clues on the other side.

4. The clues are: **Pico**-means there is one number right but it is in the wrong place. **Fermi**-means there is one number right and it is in the right place. **Bagels**-means that there are no numbers right at all in their guess. (Explain to them that **Bagels** is a very good clue to get and show them why the first few times). Give double clues if two numbers are correct but in the wrong place, i.e. pico, pico.

5. The first few times this is played it is a good idea to walk the group through the process of guessing by having the numbers 0-9 on the board also. Help them see the process of elimination by actually erasing or crossing out the numbers that are not usable after each guess. Circle those numbers that may be possible answers.

		Numbers Guessed	Clues
(The number is 78)		1. 16	Bagels
	Number	2. 84	Pico
		— —	

✗ 2 3 ④ 5 ✗ 7 ⑧ 9 0

X = No   ◯ = could be

6. Start with an unlimited number of guesses. When they have grasped the idea, limit them to 10 guesses.

Comments: Children learn a strategy of elimination and of logical reasoning.

This game is a lot of fun. Be sure to validate each child's guess somehow, such as "good guess" or "OK, that guess will help eliminate these numbers."

Half Logic or Higher/Lower   For Grades: 1 - 5

Purpose: A very good beginning number game that teaches the strategy of halving number columns, and the concept of elimination.

Materials: Large paper and pen or chalkboard and chalk.

Procedure:

1. List the numbers 1-25 on the paper or board in a column. Increase the list as the children gain confidence.

2. Have children sit in front of the writing surface.

3. Tell them that this is a guessing game. You are hiding a number that falls between 1-25 and the children must figure out the number by asking questions.

4. They cannot guess specific numbers, but must ask if the hidden number is higher or lower; for example, is it higher than 15? The teacher can only answer yes or no. (Asking if a number is between two others gets tricky; save that for later).

5. The teacher can also say, "That was a good question," because there is a strategy to guessing that you want them to figure out.

6. Play the game without telling them what the strategy is for a while. Then, ask them if they have noticed it.

7. When a child guesses in a way that eliminates a large block of numbers, call it to the group's attention and ask them why it was a good question.

8. The strategy this game is looking for is cutting the column in half each time a question is asked, reducing the quantity of numbers to be considered each time.

9. After the group has tried this several times, tell them that now it is a contest between the teacher and them. If they guess the number in less than ten questions, they get a point; if not, then the teacher gets a point. Keep score, and have fun! As they get more adept at this, reduce the number of allowable guesses for increased challenge.

Comments: A group that has developed this strategy will be able to get a number in less than 5-6 questions. It becomes an exciting challenge to "beat the teacher," no matter how many numbers are used.

Building a Better Bathtub   For Grades: K - 8

Purpose: To warm up a group, provide inclusion for all children; demonstrate the fun and power of brainstorming as a technique for solving problems.

Materials: Large piece of paper and marking pen for each team.

Procedure:

1. Break group into teams of four (fewer if your group is small).

2. Provide each team with large paper and a marking pen.

3. Tell them that each team is going to design a better bathtub.

4. They need to select one member of each team to write down the ideas.

5. They are to discuss what would work by taking turns around their table and writing every idea down as quickly as possible, without comment or judgment. Encourage ideas that are offbeat and unique. They have five minutes for this part.

6. Stop the teams after 5 minutes.

7. Next, they are to discuss the ideas individually, clarify any confusing ones, allowing each person to explain their idea. This part should take 10 minutes. Allow every team member a turn in sequence.

8. Stop the teams again and tell them that they will now vote on the ideas they want to keep in their bathtub. They will read each idea and vote it up or down. Majority vote wins. Items not making it are crossed out. This should take another 5 minutes.

9. Bring the group back together to present their finished ideas for a better bathtub.

10. Discuss the whole process. How did they feel doing it? Were some of the ideas silly? Was it hard not to comment or criticize ideas? Was it fun?

11. This can be done with any type of machine.

Comments: This activity was adapted from *Tribes*; see page 77 for publishing information.

Geography Game   For Grades: 2 - 7

Purpose: To reinforce the concept of direction, cardinal and relative.

Space: Use a large square-shaped area that has room for running. Preferably, about the length of a basketball court (squared) is good, although the width will work also for younger children. A kickball diamond is fine for younger children, but too small for older runners.

Procedure:

Mark the boundaries of your running space. Point the edges out to the students by walking to each line and stating which direction you are standing in, "Now I am "north," "south," "east," west," or "Marin, San Jose, Oakland, Ocean Beach." (Whatever cities or landmarks are relevant to your area.)

Start with the children in a row on one of the lines. Ask them, "Where are you now?" Make sure they remember all the location names.

When you call out a direction - the children run to that locale, behind the line you designated. They run at the same time, but they run individually, unless you give the following directions:

1. Carpool - this is three people running together, holding hands to make a row. The three must cross the line together as a team.

2. Rainstorm - this means they must stop and two students will make a shelter (like "London Bridge"), and the third person must get under the shelter. They do not continue to their designation until you tell them to move again. (i.e. "Continue to San Jose.") (This can be walking).

3. Earthquake! - This means they must stop instantly, assume the duck and cover position wherever they are. Any child not in duck and cover, (for example - sprawled out on the ground), does not survive the earthquake. They must go sit on the sidelines. They are "out."

4. Other possibilities will suggest themselves depending on major weather or conditions in your region: i.e. "hurricane!" or "tornado!"

Explain the rules and play the game with a practice the first time. No one is out while learning the rules.

Now they are ready for the "real game." You call a direction. The children follow your direction. The **last** person or group to either cross the line or get into correct formation is out of the game and sits on the sidelines. Continue until there are only 3 or 6 players left. This insures carpool and rainstorm possibilities, and helps make it not quite so competitive.

Comments: There is usually time for several games an activity period, so "out" children get another chance. The game can be modified for younger children by changing the size of the space and using easily recognizable designations: i.e. blue line, bench.

Bumper Sticker   For Grades: 2 - 8

Purpose: To encourage listening skills; to include every child.

Materials: Long thin paper, about 4" x 10", marking pens or crayons.

Procedure:

1. Sit children at tables and provide them each with paper and writing tools.

2. They are to make a bumper sticker of their own choice out of the paper. Give them about 10-15 minutes.

3. Have each child share his or her bumper sticker with the class. Take volunteers at first.

4. Put the papers up where they can be seen by every one and give time to read them all.

5. Go around the group and ask each person to tell which ones they might actually use, which ones surprised them, which ones they like best. Discuss the purpose that each bumper sticker seems to express such as a point of view, advertisement or communication.

Comments: This activity adds a different perspective to the group. It is fun and imaginative, and often surprising.

Logic Grids

These are language-oriented games that involve the use of a grid to plot given information. They are designed to enhance logical reasoning skills. Children love these problems and develop increasing skill with them as the problems contain more information and variables. Once you have the idea of how they work, you and the children can design your own with subjects and information that are relevant to your school or neighborhoods. The children can give their problems to the others to solve.

Example: Nancy, Jerry, Jan and Rob are all artists. One of them uses only felt pens, one uses only watercolors, one uses only crayons, and one uses only black pencils. Find out what each person uses with these clues:

1. Jan loves to use bright colors, but does not like felt pens.

2. Rob and Jan never have paint on their hands, but their friend does.

3. Nancy takes very good care of her brushes.

4. Jerry thinks black pencils are boring.

Children use the grid to plot the information and to see the solution more easily. X out the non-possible choices. There are many of these types of problems available, and inventing their own is quite a challenge for children.

	felt pens	water colors	crayons	black pencils
Nancy				
Jerry				
Jan				
Rob				

Logic Grid

Brain Teasers

These word problems contain a twist that makes figuring out the answer a bit tricky. There are several sources for these problems, including some textbooks. These are fun to do as a whole group, or in teams to see which can figure it out first.

Sample: Two mothers and two daughters each won a prize at the fair in the baseball throw booth. These were the last three prizes given away at that booth that day. How is that possible? *Answer:* There was a grandmother, mother and daughter.

Start with simpler ones and work the children into the more complex. Some teachers present these, but usually as homework or as an aside, so some of the older children may have experienced some of the questions.

Spontaneous Problems

The idea of the spontaneous problem is to allow the children to use their imagination freely to create unusual solutions in a given time limit. This encourages flexibility and teamwork. The ideas presented were originated by *Odyssey of the Mind*, a competition of problem-solving skills for children of all ages.

Spontaneous Problem #1:

A Long Paper   For Grades: 3 - 5

Materials: One piece 5 1/2" X 8 1/2" paper, scissors, and small piece of tape for each child.

Procedure:

1. Time limit: 30 minutes.

2. Tell students: You have a piece of paper 5 1/2" x 8 1/2", scissors and a small piece of tape. You are to cut the paper any way you want, and then tape one edge to the floor. You will extend the paper as far as it will reach without breaking. All students will extend their paper at the same time. They must complete the cutting before any extension takes place. If the paper breaks, where it broke is the distance scored.

Comments: This activity stirs up a lot of interest, discussion and creative thinking, as well as friendly competition.

Spontaneous Problem #2:

Soap   **For Grades: 2 - 5**

Procedure:

1. Time Limit — one minute to think, two minutes to respond for each team.

2. Tell children — They have a million bars of soap. What unusual things can they do with them? They get one point for every response, three for those that are interesting or creative.

3. Divide them into teams of four. The points are given to the teams.

4. Teams must not discuss ahead of time.

5. Teams answer in sequence, one answer per teammate, and may not skip turns or repeat or pass.

6. If a team member is stuck, the whole team is stuck.

7. Once time is started, it will not be stopped.

8. The opinion of the judge is subjective and final.

Comments: Quick thinking games like this one are fun, fast and very exhilarating for many children. As they get used to doing this type of problem they begin to understand the pace and the criteria. Team spirit develops with encouragement and discussion afterwards. Was it hard? Did you get frustrated? What did you like about it? Invent questions for them, and let them invent questions for each other.

Science

After-school programs have the opportunity to offer hands-on and exciting science programs and have choices in how they want to plan and present science activities. Some after-school program teachers may be initially uncomfortable presenting science, other than nature study. Starting with nature study is fine, because when children observe the natural occurences around them they are beginning their science awareness.

Many after-school programs have a table set up for nature-type items. These tables may contain bugs, small animals, leaves, rocks and shells. This is an excellent idea and themes can be expanded to include things such as crystals, magnets, mold, optical illusions, magnifying glasses, microscopes, seasonal objects and pictures, snakes, space, environments (like deserts or forests), and plants and sprouts. The items on the table should change regularly (about every 2-3 weeks) and be set up to allow touching whenever reasonable. A background of posters or *National Geographic* pictures is an excellent addition to this area. There are impressive nature study books available with wonderful ideas for a table or corner. A science table helps the children focus on science that is everywhere around them, and helps teach observation skills. The items and pictures lead the children to notice, explore and question, vital ingredients in any science program.

However, this type of table area should not be all there is to a science program. Science is also the process of finding answers by making, observing, experimenting and researching. Adults often feel uneasy presenting the more technical areas of scientific inquiry, and this is reflected in their science offerings. It is necessary for children to explore things like batteries, wires, chemicals and parts of appliances. They need hands-on experiments and opportunities to deviate from the standard texts if the process of exploration takes them that way.

To create more dynamic science learning in the after-school program teachers can:

• confer with classroom teachers and enhance and deepen students experiences and knowledge in areas that are being covered in the classroom;

• develop lessons in topic areas that classroom teachers might not have time to cover;

• focus after-school science activities within the "Investigation and Experimentation" standards and skills category.

Suggestions for Science Projects

• Do science projects in small groups of 10 children or less.

• Allow each group to experiment at least once every week to two weeks.

• Promote questioning and exploring.

• Make your experiments as hands-on as possible.

• Do an activity in advance, so you know what to expect.

• Allow children to deviate.

• Stress observation skills as a scientific tool.

Some good ways to start experimenting:

1. Find appliances that are no longer working such as calculators, TV's, radios, and battery-operated toys. Remove the electrical cords prior to investigating. Have the children dismantle them. Provide pliers and different size Phillips and flathead screwdrivers. Battery-operated toys have little motors in them that are great to discover and watch turn, after they have been dissected from the toy. Caution: be sure to remove the batteries and check for battery acid in the toys.

2. Put an "Experimentation table" outside. Set the following items and utensils in containers, on the table. Provide empty containers for combining them.

   • Mix vinegar and baking soda, or oil and water.

   • Stir and blow food coloring and soap with straws.

   • Put out colored water, vinegar and oil to see what mixes, sinks or floats.

- Set up straws, funnels, and measuring cups or rulers, tape and items to measure, to see relationships.

3. Allow the children to "play" with the items on the table.

4. Help steer their focus into observing and commenting on what is happening when things are combined. Ask questions that allow for discussion or further observation such as:

- What is happening to the baking soda?

- Where do you think the tiny bubbles are coming from?

- What do you see?

- What do they do when you mix them?

- Can you find something else that does the same thing?

Science Resources

There is an easy-to-use series of science activity books by Janice Van Cleave, published by John Wiley and Sons, Inc. Titles include: *Science Around the Year, Chemistry for Every Kid, Physics for Every Kid,* and *Biology for Every Kid.*

The EXPLORATORIUM, an interactive science musuem in San Francisco, has put together a set of books they call "Snack Books" that are full of fun and engaging science experiments and projects. Written by Paul Doherty and Don Rathen, published by John Wiley and Sons. **www.exploratorium.edu**

Lawrence Hall of Science in Berkeley, CA publishes an exciting science program with their GEMS guides, FOSS kits, and many other science activity items. **www.lhs.berkeley.edu**

Rainmaking   For Grades K-6

Purpose: To observe change from liquid to gas, and back again.

Materials: A cookie sheet, a saucepan or teakettle, a heat source, another pan or pot to catch the "rain." **Optional:** drawing of the rain cycle (see diagram)

Set Up:

1. Fill saucepan or teakettle with water.

2. Discuss with the children how some things change when heat is applied. Can they think of things that do? (Baked goods, snow water).

3. Remind them that observation is the key to science.

Procedure:

1. Heat the teakettle or pan until the water is slowly boiling.

2. Hold the cookie sheet over the water high enough so the steam can rise and form drops on the bottom. Ask them, "What is happening now?"

3. As the steam condenses, it will begin to fall off the cookie sheet and land on the object you have strategically placed beneath it.

4. Add ice to the pot and start over. What happens? Does it take longer? Does it work?

5. Show them the rain cycle drawing and discuss how the experiment follows the same plan — heating, evaporating, condensing and falling.

Comments: This simple experiment is primarily teacher-directed and stresses observation skills. Promote discussion throughout it to increase the group's involvement. Slightly tilting the cookie sheet will help the "rain" fall where you want it to land.

Colored Drops   For Grades: 2 - 6

Purpose: To develop observation skills.

Materials: Red and green food coloring, eye droppers, liquid water softener, waxed paper, pencils, and water.

Set Up:

1. Before beginning, mix red food coloring and a small amount of water together, to make bright red. Then mix green food coloring and water together with one or two drops of water softener. Have this ready before the children sit down. The red should drop onto waxed paper in a firm dome; the green should fall flat and run.

2. Divide the children into groups of two. Provide each group with three 6" x 6" pieces of waxed paper and two pencils.

Procedure:

1. Give each team half an eyedropper of the red mixture. Allow them to roll it, touch it with the pencils and/or their fingers, wiggle the paper and smell it. Ask for comments.

2. Put the waxed paper with the red aside for a few minutes, and give them the same amount of green mix. Allow time for observation and comments. How does this compare to the red? Have the children put a little of the green onto a red drop. What happens? (The red will flatten out right away).

3. Ask the children to predict which mixture acts most like regular water.

4. Give them half a dropper of regular water on the third waxed paper sheet. (It acts like red mix). Give time to observe and compare.

5. Allow time for investigation. Try the experiment on other types of surfaces. Discuss what happened and explain the difference in how the mixes were made. Ask the children what they think water softener does. How does water act differently on waxed and unwaxed paper? What is the waxed paper good for and how does water softener help?

Comments: The water softener breaks up the surface tension of the water and flattens it.

Liquids, Solids & Gases   For Grades: K - 4

Purpose: Classification by property

Materials: Three plastic baggies per student, twist ties to close them, pencils, and solid and liquid substances.

Set Up:

1. Take one baggie and fill it with a solid material (i.e. a rock), another with water, and leave the third for later.

2. Have the children sit in a circle and talk with you for a few minutes.

Procedure:

1. Show the solid baggie and have the children describe it. Demonstrate the properties.

Properties of solids are:

- Do not change shape easily
- Are usually visible
- Another solid cannot easily pass through it

2. Show the liquid baggie and have them describe it. Add a little food coloring to help them see movement.

Properties of liquids are:

- Can change shape easily
- Can be visible or invisible
- Solids can pass through it easily (show this)

3. Show them the third empty baggie. What is in it? (Nothing). Blow into it. What is in it now? (Air). Air is a gas. Can you see it? Does it change shapes? Open the bag and describe it with their help.

Properties of gases are:

- Can change shape easily
- Usually invisible (polluted air is not)
- Solids pass through easily

4. Let the children collect their own substances. Have them show their bags and tell why they classified them as liquid, solid or gas.

5. Make a long list of possible liquids, gases and solids. (Watch out for glass, and for silly putty; those are tricky to classify.)

Alka-Seltzer™ Testing   For Grades: 3 - 5

Purpose: Observation of properties

Materials: For every two children: one Alka-Seltzer™ tablet, 2 clear plastic cups (or other container), hand magnifying glass, matches or a candle, small paper (white and dark colored), pencils, water, one glass test tube, spoons (optional). For the teacher: a large sheet of paper and marking pen or chalkboard.

Set Up:

1. Divide the children into pairs and pass out the materials.

2. In preparation for experimentation have the children fill a plastic cup one third full of water and have it at their place.

Procedure:

1. Tell the children they are going to investigate the properties of the Alka-Seltzer™. Caution the children that the tablets are medicine and not to be eaten. Place the unused tablets well out of reach.

2. Write the possible properties on the board or a large sheet of paper. ("Properties" means the important characteristics of any substance, i.e. color, weight (density), hardness, smell, feel, taste, does it dissolve? etc.)

3. Ask the children to break the tablet into four sections.

4. Take a quarter tablet and crush it onto a piece of dark paper with fingers or a spoon. Look at the crushed pieces with the magnifying glass. Notice the differences in the shapes and sizes of the pieces. Have them draw what they see (powder and crystals).

5. Next, put a quarter tablet into the test tube and fill it one fourth full of water. Have the children put their fingers over the top and feel what is escaping (gas). Also, have them feel the bottom of the tube. (It will feel cold because heat energy is required to help the reaction occur. The water cools as the tablet dissolves).

6. Put a quarter tablet into a cup and cover it just barely with water. Light a match and hold it over the escaping gas without touching the water. What happens to the flame? (Carbon dioxide is created by the dissolving tablet, the CO_2 escapes, and puts out the flame). Repeat this after a few minutes with the same cup. Now what happens to the flame? (The CO_2 is gone, and the match burns). (A candle provides a somewhat safer flame for this part, but the wax tends to drip into the seltzer).

7. Let the children play with and investigate the last quarter tablet on their own. Tell them they can taste it if they want. Tell them to write down what they notice.

8. Discuss the experiments as a group and write properties they observed on the paper or board. What worked? What did not?

Comments: For variation, try different types of Alka-Seltzer™.

Soap Plant   For Grades: K - 6

Purpose: To demonstrate natural uses for plants, and integrate concepts from both Social Studies and Science.

Materials: Blueblossom (Ceanothus Thyrsiflorus — see illustration), water, towels, several bowls.

Set Up:

1. If you want to compare the dried blossoms with the fresh, you will need to pick at least one stalk per child about a week ahead of time. When gathering the blossoms, pinch or cut the plant carefully at the end of the flower head. Pick the same quantity of fresh blossoms for each child, plus a couple of extra blossoms.

2. To dry, lay the blossoms out on a clean, dry surface. Be sure they are not touching each other. When dry (about 5 days), strip all of the flowers off the stems and put them back out to dry for another two days.

3. Put bowls, towels and pitchers of water on a table or other large flat surface. If there are not many children, you can use a sink instead. Doing it on a table allows large groups to do this project.

4. Divide the children into groups depending on how many bowls you have. There should be two bowls for each group - one bowl with warm water, one bowl with cold water. Have a bucket of rinse water set aside for washing hands.

Procedure:

1. Discuss the fact that early people on all continents, including Native Americans, used wild plants for different uses. Discuss with the children some ideas on how different plants can be used. Give the children both the common and technical names for the plant you are using.

2. Demonstrate by dipping your hands into water, then rubbing a fresh blossom head briskly between both hands. If there are no suds, use more water and rub harder. These blossoms can get really sudsy!

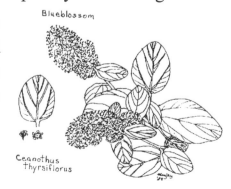

Blueblossom

Ceanothus
thyrsiflorus

3. Look at the fresh blossoms and the dried ones and have children comment on the differences. Hypothesize which will create more suds. Take a prediction vote and write results down for later comparison.

4. The children should each have a chance to try fresh and dried blossoms, and warm and cold water.

5. Have the group discuss their observations. What happened? Which combination worked best? Why was the cold water important? (In history, people often bathed in the streams and rivers). Is this soap ecological? Why were the dried blossoms important? (During the winter months there were no fresh blossoms available).

Comments: Ceanothus has shiny green leaves and clusters of blossoms, either white or bluish. It is often used as a landscape decoration and is easily found. Ask the property owner or park officials where you want to pick the blossoms for permission; they may allow you to return every year. This project can be the beginning of integrating Science and Social Studies, or a study of the Native Americans, State History or an introduction to Ecology. Many other members of the Ceanothus family were used all across the United States. Amole soap root is another excellent sudsy plant, but much less accessible in large quantities.

Chemical Gardens   For Grades: 3 - 5

Purpose: To observe changes.

Materials: Laundry bluing (Caution: this stains certain materials), water, salt, ammonia (**Caution:** avoid inhalation and if skin comes in contact with the ammonia, carefully rinse the skin with water), charcoal, pieces of old bricks, rocks, sponges, foil or glass pie tins, food coloring, measuring cups, empty containers.

Set-Up:

1. Divide the children into groups of 3 or 4.

2. Give each group several rocks, sponges, pieces of charcoal and bricks, three pie tins or plates, and an empty container.

3. Put the bluing, ammonia, water, salt, and measuring cups in a central, easily monitored spot. This area should be well supervised.

Procedure:

1. Have each group arrange their pie tins with charcoal, bricks or rocks. Some groups may want to have one tin with only charcoal, one tin with only brick, etc.; others may want a variety. Allow freedom to mix and match.

2. An adult should be present during all pouring and mixing. A representative from each group goes to the "mixing area." They put 1/4 cup ammonia, 1/4 cup salt, 1/4 cup bluing and 1/4 cup warm water together into their empty container. (A quarter cup is 4 Tablespoons).

3. The mixture is poured over the tins evenly.

4. Another representative gets the food coloring and drops a few drops onto each piece of rock, brick, sponge or charcoal.

5. Put the tins in a safe spot to sit overnight. In the next day or so, they will be covered with what looks like colored moss.

6. Have the children observe which substance has the most "moss" and which grows the fastest. Slowest? Which does not grow well? Discuss possible reasons why or why not. (The "moss" is the solidification of the chemicals in combination).

Comments: Charcoal will absorb more mixture than the bricks, and the rocks will not absorb much at all, unless you use a sandstone type. Try this experiment with other things as bases, such as shells, tiles, terracotta, pottery shards.

Corn Popping   For Grades: K - 6

Purpose: To note that heat can change things; corn contains moisture.

Materials: Popcorn kernels, matches, cooking oil, several eye droppers, one test tube for every two children, one clothes pin per test tube, small pieces of aluminum foil (one 2"x2", another 4"x4") for each pair, one candle per pair.

Set Up:

1. Set several eyedroppers and a container of oil to one side.

2. Tell the children they are going to observe changes made by heat.

3. Explain safety rules for using candles.

4. Pass out materials; give each pair of children a test tube, matches, one piece of both sizes of foil, three or four kernels of corn, one clothespin and one candle.

5. Demonstrate how to attach the clothespin onto the tube, or have it already done for them (see diagram). Also state that the test tubes should never be pointed toward anyone.

Procedure:

1. Ask the children if the corn is moist or dry. Take a vote.

2. Show them how to fold the small foil piece to make a cover for the tube. Set it to one side.

3. Light the candle and drip some wax onto the large foil piece. Set the candle into the melted wax until it firms. This will hold the candle steady during the experiment.

4. Have one team member put a drop of oil into the tube.

5. Put one corn kernel into the tube and put the foil cover over the top. Put the tube over the flame, but keep it one inch above the flame. (If the tube gets into the flame it will turn black, but it can be cleaned when cool).

6. With the clothespin, hold the test tube over the flame, and move it gently back and forth through the heat. What is happening inside the tube? (As

the seed heats up, the moisture inside it escapes as steam and goes to the top and sides of the tube).

7. When the corn pops, blow out the candle and shake the popcorn out.

8. Have the group discuss what changed. Was it fast or slow? Where did the moisture come from? Why did the corn pop? (The moisture is heated and turns to steam and exerts pressure on the outer layer of the kernel. When the outer layer breaks, the corn pops immediately). Ask why some did not pop. (There was a crack in the outer layer and the moisture would have dried already). Is the corn heavier when it is popped?

Comments: Let the children try popping with no lid; with more than one kernel in the tube; with different types of corn. Try this with a raisin. (Stop the heating process before the raisin burns). How is this different?

Stereo Hangers   For Grades: K - 6

Purpose: Sound travels through metal, string and fingers. Stereo means from two directions at the same time.

Materials: 1 roll of thread, 1 metal hanger, two paper cups and a pencil per child.

Set Up:

1. Ask each child to bring a metal hanger.

2. Build your own stereo hanger first so you know how it works (see diagram).

Procedure:

1. Pass out two cups to each child.

2. Cut 2 pieces of thread 1 1/2 feet long. Tie one piece of thread to each end of the hanger. This part is ready. Have children wrap a few inches of the thread around the first joint of the index finger of both hands. Put both fingers into ears and lean over with the hanger dangling down. Tap the hanger gently on a table or other surface. Each child will hear the vibrations separately. Have children make sound for each other by running fingers over the thread in patterns.

3. Put a small hole in the middle of the bottom of the paper cup. String the thread through and tie securely on the inside of each cup. Now put the cups up to the ears. (The sounds are much louder).

4. Ask the children to play with the sounds with each other. Let them tap rhythms on the hanger with pencils or other things; tap the hanger over different types of objects. Remove one cup from an ear (no stereo). Have someone hold the thread after the hanger is tapped (the vibration stops, so does the sound).

5. Try tying paper clips to the thread knots inside the cups; does that change the sound? Use another metal object on the strings to test for other possibilities.

6. Discuss how it works. Can they figure it out? (The hanger vibrates when struck, the vibrations travel up the strings, the string vibrating causes the air in the ear to vibrate on the eardrum, producing what each child hears).

Comments: Try to record this with a tape recorder if available. Put the microphone into the cup for best results. Can they make "music"?

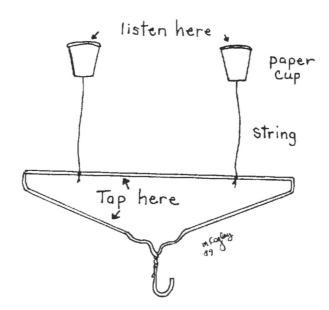

Battery Circuits   For Grades: 2 - 6

Purpose: Familiarity with batteries as electricity, circuits as electrical pathways, bulbs as part of circuits, introduction of "negative and positive poles."

Materials: Large drawing of a bulb to show entire group.
Per group of children:1 D battery, 1 strip of foil 5"x1" (or electrical thin wire), one 3-volt flashlight bulb, two pieces of masking tape, one rubber band.

Set Up:

1. Make the drawing of the bulb in advance (see diagram).

2. Divide the children into teams.

3. Pass out the materials to each team.

Procedure:

1. Ask the children to describe the battery. What is written on it at the top and bottom? Which one says negative and positive? How do you know? What is it made of (cardboard, metal)? How is a battery used? Why?

2. Go through the same process with the bulb. Is the small wire (filament) connected to anything? (Yes). How is it shaped? Do the large wires touch? Can you see where the larger wires are attached?

3. Tell them to use the materials available and try to make the bulb light up. Draw each attempt, even if it does not work. How many ways can they find that will work? Let an exchange of ideas happen, including failed efforts.

4. Attempts that bypass the bulb, but produce heat on the foil strip will be a "short circuit," and will wear out the battery. Have the children observe that the foil will get hot quickly.

5. Allow enough time and then discuss their efforts. Sharing information is an important part of science. Both successful and failed attempts are valuable learning experiments; discuss them all.

Comments: Make a diagram of what worked and what did not for use in later experimentation.

Masks

Making masks is a traditional art form. Many ethnic groups use masks for ceremonies and celebrations. Children enjoy pretending to be someone or something else. A good way to achieve this is by wearing masks. There are many ways to create masks, from paper bags and plates to plaster casts of faces. Masks can be worn for dress-up, in plays, in parades, and can be hung up to decorate walls.

Ice Cream Carton Masks

Materials: 3-gallon ice cream cartons, masking tape, scissors, variety of cardboard tubes and rolls, tempera paint, glue and decorations such as feathers, pipe cleaners, straws, glitter, ribbons, and yarn.

Set-up:

1. Ask your local ice cream store to save containers or ask the children to bring them in.

2. If there is a metal rim on the top of the cartons, carefully pry it off. The lid of the carton is not needed but can be cut up for decorations.

3. Set out the materials on the art table.

Procedure:

1. Some ideas for masks are a robot, monster, space creature, Hopi Kachina Doll (show pictures as examples), African Masks from different nations (show pictures as examples), ogre and different animals.

2. Using a sharp scissors, cut holes for eyes, nose and mouth. They can be any shape or size depending on what the mask will be.

3. The cardboard tubes can be used for pop-out eyes, nose, ears, or other objects. Cut the tube to the size needed and then cut four 1 inch slits, equidistant on the bottom of the tube. Fold them outwards making a platform (see diagram).

4. Tape the tube securely onto the carton so that it is sticking out.

5. Use pipe cleaners, straws, feathers or other objects to make horns, antenna and head dresses.

6. When all the pop-out items are secured, paint the mask using a variety of colors and shapes.

7. Decorate in any fashion.

8. When the mask is finished, have the child try it on. If it is too low, stuff the top with newspaper. If it does not rest comfortably on his or her shoulders, cut out sections on either side of the carton for shoulder rests.

Plastic Bottle Masks

Materials: Milk, bleach or other plastic bottles with handles, sharp scissors, glue, decorations such as yarn, foil, glitter, fabric, pipe cleaners, buttons, and marking pens.

Set-up:

1. Cut the back of the container to the handle; do not cut the handle and leave the pour spout intact (see diagram).

2. Set out a wide range of decorations for the children to choose from.

Procedure:

1. Have the children draw eyes and mouth on the mask.

2. Puncture a hole in the mask and carefully cut out the eyes and mouth.

3. Decorate – the wilder the better!

Comments: Paint will not stick well on these bottles.

Plaster Masks

Materials: Plaster of Paris strips, Vaseline, water, a shallow container, paint, head bands or hair fasteners and decorations

Set-up:

1. Cut the plaster strips into 2 to 3 inch long pieces.

2. Purchase or borrow hair fasteners or head bands to keep children's hair away from their faces.

3. It is best to have an adult put the first mask on a child or another adult, to show the children the process. Then the remaining children should choose partners (one creates the mask on the other and then they change places). When children put masks on other children it encourages cooperation and allows for many children to participate at once.

Procedure:

1. Fasten hair back, completely away from forehead.

2. Have the child wearing the mask put Vaseline all over his or her face (excluding eyes and lips).

3. Be sure that an adult puts the first mask on a child's face to demonstrate.

4. Place the strips of plaster in the water, and run between two fingers to remove excess water.

5. Gently place the strip on the child's face and smooth down.

6. Leave holes for eyes and mouth.

7. Make sure the strips are placed slightly overlapping and so that no skin shows through.

8. Let the mask dry on the child's face for about 20 minutes. It may itch a bit.

9. Carefully lift the mask off the child's face and let dry overnight.

10. Decorate any way you wish. Paint, feathers and glitter make a wonderful mask!

Papier-Mâché Masks

Materials: Newspaper, papier-mâché paste or liquid starch, a round balloon, masking tape, a container to set the balloon in, egg carton, scissors, heavy string or ribbon, and paint.

Set-up:

1. Make sure the balloon is large enough to fit as a mask.

2. Blow up the balloon.

3. Prepare the papier-mâché paste (see recipe section) or use liquid starch.

Procedure:

1. If the child wants a nose or other parts to stick out, cut up egg cartons and tape them onto the balloon.

2. Follow the directions for Balloon Piñata in the 3-dimensional art section; making sure to cover the entire surface.

3. Let dry.

4. Pop the balloon and cut it in half (see diagram).

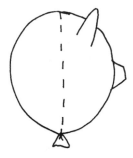

5. Punch a hole on each side for tying a string to secure the mask on the child's head.

6. Paint and decorate in any manner.

Paper Bag Masks

Materials: Grocery-sized paper bag, scissors, glue, markers, decorations.

Set-up:

1. Set out a paper bag for each child.

2. Put a variety of materials for decorations such as glitter, markers, ribbon, yarn, lace, and pipe cleaners.

Procedure:

1. Each child slips the paper bag over his or her head.

2. Have another child mark the places where the child's eyes, nose, and mouth are.

3. Take the bag and draw a face on the mask, using the marks as a guide.

4. Cut out eyes, nose and mouth.

5. Decorate the mask. Fringe can be cut out and glued on.

Comments: Paper bags are also great for fast costumes.

Paper Plate Masks

Materials: Paper plates, fabric, sharp scissors, masking tape, glue or a glue gun, a wooden stick or rod, and decorations.

Set-up:

1. If a glue gun is being used, supervise carefully.

2. Place the paper plates, fabric and scissors out on the art table.

Procedure:

1. Choose a piece of fabric to cover the paper plate.

2. Trace the plate on the fabric, cut it out and glue the material to the plate (a glue gun works best).

3. Let the glue dry.

4. Cut holes for the eyes, nose, and mouth.

5. Add other details and decorations such as ears, yarn hair, ribbons, material, glitter, or pipe cleaners for antenna.

6. Attach the wooden stick or rod to the back of the plate with masking tape or glue for a handle.

Comments: These make old-fashioned masks. They are fun to create and work well for dramatic play, when presenting a favorite story, school plays, special events and shows.

African Style Masks

Materials: Grocery-sized paper bags, crayons, scissors, brushes and thin black paint.

Set-up:

1. Mix the black paint with water to create a wash.

2. Cut an oval the size of a face, out of the front of each paper bag.

3. Show the children pictures of traditional African masks to give them ideas for designs. Show them a variety of masks from the many African nations and let the children decide which style they wish to make.

Procedure:

1. Draw shapes for the eyes, nose, and mouth, and cut them out.

2. Color the face of the mask with designs, pressing very hard with the crayons, (geometric lines, wiggles, and shapes work well).

3. Paint the wash of black paint over the mask, making long, even strokes.

4. Let the ovals dry.

5. Cut the four "edges" of the oval. Pull each "edge" back and staple the cut areas (see diagram).

7. The cuts will give the mask a 3 dimensional look.

8. Attach string for wearing as a mask or to hang on the wall.

1. Mask before cutting   2. Making the cuts   3. Stapling cut area   4. Mask after folding and stapling

Puppets

Putting on a puppet show is delightful for children of all ages. There are many ways to create both puppets and a stage, ranging from quite simple to rather complex. Allowing children to make up their own puppets and show is a wonderful learning experience.

Performing a puppet show in front of an audience gives children a chance to develop many kinds of new skills. Some puppet shows take much planning; others can be spontaneous. For planned puppet shows, there are many roles to fill including: writing or choosing the show, creating the puppets, memorizing the dialogue, planning and making the props and scenery, building the puppet stage and drawing invitations or announcements. Using music in a puppet show is a wonderful way to liven it up. The children in our program performed a puppet show that they chose from a favorite book. They made up an original song to go along with the dialogue.

Puppet shows provide an excellent opportunity for children to use their imaginations and develop creativity. They are fun projects for interest groups, clubs or thematic units. Shy children often blossom with a puppet.

Ideas for making stages

Large boxes make impressive puppet stages. Cut a big opening in the front for the stage. Paint and decorate the outside. Suspend the box between two tables; or for marionettes, cut another hole in the top and drop the puppets down. Scenery can be either painted on the back of the box or drawn on rolls of paper. Put one wooden rod on either side of the puppet stage. Attach the scenery paper on both rods so that the different backgrounds can be rolled by. Make curtains out of material over a rope or dowel and tack or tie onto outside or front of the stage. Draping material over a table or a doorway makes an instant puppet stage.

A shadow puppet show only takes a few minutes to set up. Tie a sheet across a wall, doorway or from posts. Place a light behind the object to be silhouetted and focus the light toward the back of the sheet. Puppets can be cut out of paper shapes or made with hands. For example, sticking up two fingers makes a bunny, or holding out arms and two fingers makes a crocodile with a mouth that opens and closes. Paper shapes should be taped, glued or stapled to a Popsicle stick or tongue depressor.

Ideas for making puppets

Decorate puppets with:

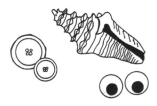

Buttons, acorns, seashells, macaroni, beads, beans, wiggle eyes, yarn, straw, raffia, feathers, felt, material, cotton balls or sequins.

Paper cups:
Decorate a paper cup for the body; use either clay or a Styrofoam ball attached to a Popsicle stick for the head. Make a slit or hole in the bottom of the cup; put the Popsicle stick end though it and you have a pop-up puppet.

Socks, gloves or mittens:
Take old socks, mittens or gloves and
sew, stuff, or cut to create hand puppets.

Cardboard: Cut out separate body parts such as the head,
the trunk, arms and legs. Paper plates can be used for the
body and head. Punch holes in each part and attach with
paper fasteners (see diagram). Tie long strings to the top of
the head and to both arms and legs. Suspend the strings
from a wooden rod or ruler. Decorate by cutting people or
animal heads out of magazines or use paint, material or crayons. Wiggle the stick or pull individual strings and you have
a marionette.

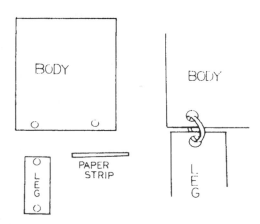

Finger Puppets: Make out of soft material or felt. Loosely trace the shape of fingers on material. Draw a border about 1/2 inches from the trace line (see diagram). Cut on the larger border, two of each finger, and sew the two matching shapes together securely. Clip the curves, seam almost to the seam, and turn inside out. Decorate with glue and small pieces of material. Paper finger puppets can be cut out and fastened around fingers. Create bodies, faces, etc.

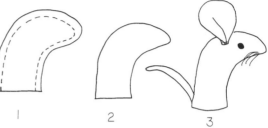

Paper bags: Stuff paper bags with newspaper; place a stick or paper-towel roll inside the bag for a handle; and tie the bag at the neck using a string or rubber band. Decorate with markers, yarn or paint.

Hands: Close fingers tightly into a ball and paint lips onto the thumb and index finger. Use either makeup, face paints or tempera paint mixed with soap. Hands can be anything from people faces, animals to scary monsters. Put acorn tops or peanut shells on fingertips and draw faces on fingers.

Wooden rods or sticks: Attach a Styrofoam or clay ball or a paper plate for the head on a wooden rod or stick. Create the face and decorate with hats, hair, ribbons, etc.

Junk and things: Puppets can be put together from all kinds of junk items and things around the house or school. Use items such as milk cartons, egg cartons, paintbrushes, feather dusters or plastic bottles. Let the children explore the many different objects they can use to make puppets!

Papier-mâché: Glue layers of paper strips onto wads of newspaper or old light bulbs to make heads for different kinds of puppets. Create arms, hands, fingers, a nose and other body parts, out of papier-mâché or fabric.

Things found in nature: Try making a puppet from things collected outdoors such as: sticks, straw, milkweeds, pussy willows, driftwood, shells and other plants.

Gifts

School-age children enjoy making gifts for family or friends. Parents cherish handmade presents. There are many gift ideas suitable for school-age children. The following pages are projects that make particularly successful gifts and allow for individual variation.

When children make special art projects to give for presents, handmade wrapping paper is the perfect finishing touch. There are several easy ways to make wrapping paper. Many forms of printing can be used on tissue paper or light paper to create wrapping paper.

Mosaic Flower Pots

Materials: Clay flower pots, ceramic tiles of various colors, tile grout, white glue, white paint, paint brushes, newspaper, a sponge and a cloth.

Set-up:

1. Cover the table with newspaper.

2. Set a flower pot, tiles, and glue with a brush out for each child. Use smaller pots for young children.

Procedure:

1. Brush a coat of white paint on the rim of the clay pot and let dry completely. (This will make the tiles stick on the pot better).

2. Paint a coat of glue on the back of each tile and place in a row on the rim. Make sure that a small space (1/8-inch) is left between each tile for the grout.

3. Continue until the entire rim is decorated with tiles. Children may want to place tiles on the body of the pot also.

4. Let dry completely.

5. Mix the grout to the consistency of mayonnaise.

6. Using rubber gloves, have the children fill in all the spaces with grout.

7. Sponge off any excess grout on body of the clay pot. Let dry for about 20 minutes and sponge off the excess grout from the tile fronts.

8. Clean the mosaic with a damp cloth after the grout has completely dried.

Egg Shell Mosaics

Materials: Broken, dyed egg shells, glue, pencils, construction paper.

Set-up:

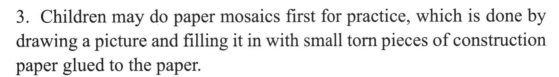

1. Break up egg shells into medium-sized pieces.

2. Place the materials on art table.

3. Children may do paper mosaics first for practice, which is done by drawing a picture and filling it in with small torn pieces of construction paper glued to the paper.

Procedure:

1. Talk to the children about mosaics and show them pictures or examples of tile mosaics.

2. Draw a picture onto the construction paper with a pencil.

3. Fill in with egg shell pieces on top of glue.

Mosaic Hot Plates

Materials: Ceramic tiles of various colors, tile grout, wood blocks, 1/4 to 3/4-inch pine molding, rubber cement, white glue, a hammer, a pencil, rubber gloves, newspaper, sponge and muffin tin.

Set-up:

1. Break up the tiles by placing them, glaze side down, between several layers of newspaper. Hit them hard with a hammer. Tile clippers can also be used.

2. Have the children sort the tiles by color and put into a muffin tin.

3. Set out a block of wood per child and start with small blocks at first. Frame the wood block with the pine molding, making sure to cut two pieces longer to overlap with the other two strips.

4. Show either an example of tile mosaic or pictures from a book.

5. This is an ongoing project, so give at least two weeks to complete.

Procedure:

1. Let the children do the egg shell mosaic project or a paper mosaic project first, to get the idea of mosaics.

2. Draw a picture onto the wood, make a very simple design. Fine lines and small details are very difficult to do.

3. Glue the tiles onto the wood with the rubber cement, making sure not to leave large holes. There should be small spaces about 1/8 inch between tiles.

4. Let dry overnight.

5. Mix the tile grout to the consistency of mayonnaise.

6. Using rubber gloves, have the children fill in all the spaces with grout.

7. Gently wipe off all the excess grout from the tiles with a sponge.

8. Let dry completely and clean the surface again with a sponge.

9. If there is grout left on the frame, it can be removed with sandpaper.

Tissue Paper Stained Glass

Materials: Sheets or scraps of tissue paper, liquid starch, glass containers (jars or bottles), paint brushes, and newspaper.

Set-up:

1. Cover the art table with newspaper.

2. Put out the tissue paper, liquid starch, and glass containers.

Procedure:

1. Cut or tear varied colors of tissue paper into small shapes.

2. Brush the tissue paper shapes onto the outside of the glass containers using the liquid starch.

3. Press down loose corners.

4. Cover glass completely with tissue paper for a stained glass effect.

Comments: A glue/water mixture can be used in place of the liquid starch. This project can also be done on paper, wood, glass or acrylic sheets, wax paper and even windows.

Lacquer Pictures

Materials: Black paint, tempera paint (bright colors), stiff paper plates, paint brushes, and white glue.

Set-up:

1. Make simple examples to show the children.

2. You may want to bring in samples of real Chinese or Japanese lacquer objects.

Procedure:

1. Paint the paper plate black and let dry, making sure there is no white showing through.

2. Create a brightly colored picture by painting over the dry black paint.

3. Let the picture dry.

4. Paint the surface with a glaze of two parts white glue and 1/2 part water.

5. Let dry and repeat the glazing daily for one week.

Comments: Fluorescent paints make a bright contrast on black backgrounds. This process can be done on pieces of wood, cardboard and other surfaces.

Crepe Paper Bottles

Materials: Sheets of colored crepe paper, scissors, glass bottles, glue, tape and an electric drill.

Set-up:

1. Take the drill bit off; it is not necessary for the project.

2. Place this activity near an electrical outlet.

3. Set up the art table with glue, crepe paper, and a bottle for each child.

Procedure:

1. Cut one-inch-wide long strips of crepe paper.

2. Tape one end of the crepe paper to the head of the drill (an adult should work the drill).

3. Have a child hold the other end of the crepe paper.

4. Turn on the drill and let it twist the paper.

5. The crepe paper will wind tightly to form a colorful rope.

6. Put glue on the bottle and wind the crepe paper rope around the bottle tightly. Start from the bottom and wind up.

Comments: This makes a wonderful vase or pencil holder. Yarn pieces can also be wound around bottles for a similar effect.

Flowers in a Jar

Materials: Baby food jars and lids, modeling clay, small dried flowers, scissors, glue and felt.

Set-up:

Set up the art table with a jar, flowers, balls of clay, and felt.

Procedure:

1. Trace the jar lid on felt and cut out.

2. Cover the outside of the jar lid with the round piece of felt (also the inside of the lid if desired).

3. Stick a ball of clay onto the inside of the lid.

4. Cut the flowers to fit inside of the jar; then press the stems into the ball of clay making a flower arrangement.

5. Put the lid onto the jar and carefully tape around the outside edge to secure the lid.

6. Set the jar upside-down so that the flowers stand up.

Comments: These are quick, easy projects and are enjoyed by all age groups. They can also be created in larger bottles or jars.

Clay Egg Holders

Materials: Clay, large and medium hard-boiled or blown eggs, acrylic paints and brushes.

Set-up:

1. Purchase clay that can either be air-dried or oven baked, or make your own clay (see Recipes Section).

2. Hard boil the eggs.

3. For blown eggs, prick a hole in the top and bottom of the eggs and blow out the insides. Set aside for use when holder is finished.

4. Prepare art table for clay work.

Procedure:

1. Make a lump of clay the size of a large egg.

2. Flatten the clay into a 3/8 inch thick oval.

3. Place a large egg in the middle of the clay.

4. Form different types of animals, objects, or people around the egg.

5. Some ideas: bear, frog, a bunny, snail, swan, nest, or person. Push clay through a garlic press to make hair, a nest or other details.

6. Remove the egg often, to make sure it does not stick to the clay, or lightly oil the egg.

7. Make sure the clay has a flat bottom and holds the egg firmly.

8. Let the clay dry without the egg, or oven bake. Most clay will shrink when dried.

9. Paint the egg holder when completely dry.

10. Dye or paint the medium-sized blown egg or hard-boiled egg, and place in the holder.

Comments: The only use for the large egg is during the making of the holder. The reason for this is because the clay shrinks when drying and will not hold a large egg. The smaller egg will actually be placed into the holder when it is dry.

Applesauce/Cinnamon Ornaments

Materials: 4 ounces ground cinnamon, 10 tablespoons applesauce, mixing bowl, wax paper, rolling pins, a spoon, acrylic paints, small paint brushes, ribbon or string, a variety of cookie cutters, rolling pins, a cookie sheet and an oven.

Set-up:

Set up places to roll out dough onto wax paper.

Procedure:

1. For Applesauce/cinnamon dough: Measure about 10 tablespoons of applesauce and put in a mixing bowl; then add about 4 ounces of ground cinnamon. Mix together with a spoon and knead into a ball. The dough should be moist, so add more applesauce, if needed. The cinnamon works like flour. Sprinkle it on the dough and rolling pin if they get sticky.

2. Roll out the dough onto the wax paper.

3. Press the cookie cutters into the dough or cut with a knife.

4. To avoid breakage keep the ornaments smaller than 4 inches.

5. Punch a hole towards the top of the ornaments, place them on the cookie sheets, and bake at 200° for 20 to 30 minutes.

7. Let cool on a wire rack.

8. Paint with acrylic paints.

9. Put string or ribbon through the hole for hanging.

Comments: These ornaments smell wonderful and should last for a few years. It also makes the school smell great! Store them in a box lined with tissue paper and keep in a cool, dry place. Tempera paint works also, but acrylic paint has more luster.

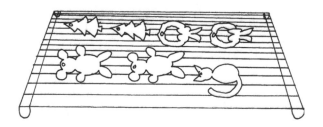

Baker's Dough Magnets

Materials: Baker's dough (see Recipes Section), acrylic paint, roll of stick-on magnets (purchase at a crafts store), cookie cutter, cookie sheets, and wax paper.

Set-up:

1. Make the Baker's dough with the children, according to recipe.

2. Put out balls of dough on wax paper.

3. Have cookie cutters or clay tools ready.

Procedure:

1. Make things out of the dough either by hand or with cookie cutters.

2. When finished, place the objects carefully onto the cookie sheet.

3. Gently push a small strip of magnet into the back of the object, making it as even as possible with the edge of the dough. Be sure to put a big strip of magnet on large objects, or the magnet will not hold the dough.

4. Bake according to directions.

5. When cooled, paint the front side.

Wooden Magnets

Materials: Very small light pieces of wood (shapes work well) that are sanded (order from a crafts catalog or get from the lumber yard), a roll of stick-on magnet strips, a metal mirror or another metal surface, glue, glitter, paint, sequins or other decorations.

Set-up:

1. Put out the pieces of wood, the glue and the decorations.

2. Keep the magnet strips away from the table until the project is finished.

Procedure:

1. Pick out wooden pieces or shapes and glue them together.

2. Then decorate the wood shapes from a wide variety of materials.

3. Let them dry.

4. Cut out a piece of magnet from the roll, making sure it is large enough to hold the wooden pieces on metal.

5. Secure magnet strip to the back of the wood. Display the finished products on the mirror.

Comments: The magnets can be displayed on refrigerators at home or used to hold up art work. They sell well at crafts fairs or fundraisers.

Magnet Creatures

Materials: Empty walnut shells, magnetic strips, paint, felt, plastic eyes, glue, paper, scissors, and a hole puncher.

Set-up:

1. Crack the walnuts in halves and take out the fruit inside; it can be saved for snack time or baking projects.

2. Put out the materials and allow for free choice.

3. Cut the felt into small squares, a bit larger than the nuts.

Procedure:

1. Talk to the children about different ideas for creatures.

2. Cover the open side of the walnut with felt.

3. Glue the felt and trim the edges.

4. Decorate the top of the walnut shell to create animals, monsters, and people. Some examples are:

    a. Lady bug: Paint red and let dry; use black hole-punching for spots; draw or make wings and use wire for antennae.

    b. Cat: Paint walnut and let dry; attach eyes; draw face; use wire for whiskers; make ears from felt.

    c. Glue on many eyes; furry fabric; and paint for a monster.

5. After the creature has dried, attach a magnetic strip to the back.

Candle Making, Wax and Crayons

Candle making is very enjoyable for children. Paraffin wax can be purchased in large slabs from catalogs or hobby stores. Metal and rubber molds can also be purchased, but milk cartons and other inexpensive materials work just as well. Wicks can be bought from a hobby store or from art catalogs. The best wicks have wire inside. Be sure you use real wicks, or test your string, because some string does not burn. If you do use string, dip the pieces in wax and let dry before putting them in the candles. Below is basic information for easy candle and wax preparation; please refer to it when doing a project.

Basic Preparation Steps for Candle Making

1. Wax should be chopped into small pieces using a hammer and chisel. Children enjoy helping with the wax chopping. It is best to chop the wax in advance, because it does take time.

2. Make sure the melting of the wax is well supervised. An adult should do the pouring. Talk to the children about fire safety and explain why they must have an adult supervise them when they burn their candles at home.

3. When melting wax, it is safest to use a double boiler. Use an old pan that is large enough to fit a coffee can inside. Put about two to three inches of water inside the pan and place it on top of the burner. When the water starts to boil, place the can of wax inside. Make sure the water does not evaporate while the wax is melting.

4. Stir the wax as it melts, and do not let it get too hot. Take the wax off the boiler as soon as all the pieces are melted.

5. Crayons can be used to color the wax. Peel crayon stubs and carefully drop them into the wax while it is melting, making sure not to splash the wax. Stir the crayon stubs until the color has mixed evenly.

6. Measure the wick to about six inches longer than the mold. Wind it around a pencil or stick; place it in the center of the mold; and lay the pencil across the mold (see diagram on page 136).

7. The top layer of wax often gets an air pocket that looks like an indentation. This can be filled using warm wax.

Sand Candles

Materials: Wax, crayon stubs, a double boiler, sand, a sand table or box, foil and wicks.

Set-up:

1. Set up a double boiler and follow the directions for candle making preparation.

2. If you do not have a sand box or a sand table, line a large box with foil and fill it with sand.

3. Wet down the sand.

Procedure:

1. Have children use their hands to make a hole in the sand for the candle. Flatten the sand on the bottom or the candle will not sit up to burn; or press fingers into the sand, to make legs. Round shapes such as circles, ovals and hearts work well.

2. Melt the wax and stir in a crayon stub for color.

3. Carefully pour the wax into the sand hole.

4. Put the wick into the middle of the candle and hold up until the candle starts to harden.

5. When completely hardened, pull the candle by the wick, out of the sand.

6. Brush off the excess sand, leaving a sandy coat.

Comments: This is a fast easy candle to make. Children can experiment with different shapes and sizes. It is a good first candle making project for younger children.

Colorful Sand Candles

Materials: Wax, crayon stubs, a double boiler, wicks, colored sand (or mix powered tempera with sand or salt), baby food jars, clear plastic glasses, or cups, and pointed sticks.

Set-up:

1. Set up a double boiler and follow the directions for candle making preparation.

2. Prepare the colored sand by either purchasing colored sand at a craft supply store or making your own. Use either white sand or salt, mixed with 1/2 teaspoon of dry powered tempera paint.

3. Set out the containers.

Procedure:

1. Pour a layer of colored sand or salt into a container.

2. Tilt the container to create wavy layers of sand.

3. Continue pouring layers of colored sand or salt.

4. A pointed stick can be used to swirl the colors and mix the layers.

5. Fill the container 3/4 full.

6. Melt the wax with a crayon.

7. Push a wick into the middle of the sand and tie the end onto a pencil; rest it across the container.

8. Pour melted wax on top to seal the sand and let it harden.

Comments: To make a paperweight, use a baby food jar with a lid and follow steps 1-6 and 8. Cover the top of the lid with felt and place it on the jar. Carefully turn the jar upside down onto the lid.

Paper Cup or Milk Carton Candles

Materials: Wax, crayon stubs, waxed containers for molds, wicks, double boiler, and pencils.

Set-up:

1. Set up the double boiler and follow the directions for candle making preparation.

2. Choose a mold for the candles.

Procedure:

1. Melt the wax and add crayons for coloring.

2. Carefully pour the wax into the mold.

3. Place the wick in the center of the candle, with one end tied around the pencil and rest it on the mold.

4. After the candle has hardened, peel off the mold.

Comments: Dixie cups, paper cups, and milk cartons make good molds and the different sizes help adjust the project to the amount of wax on hand. If you use metal molds, grease them first or spray with silicon mold release. For multi-colors and layers, pour one layer and let dry, then pour the next layer until the candle is at the desired height. To make a candle with holes, pour wax over crushed ice cubes. Another variation is to make chunks of colored wax in an ice cube tray. After they harden, place them in the mold and pour slightly cooled clear wax over them.

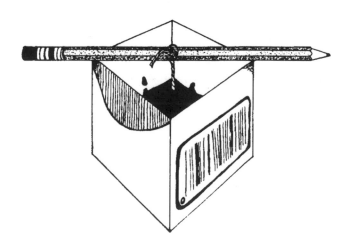

Fried Egg Candle

Materials: Wax, wicks with wire inside, a yellow crayon, a double boiler, mixing cups, stirring sticks, and aluminum foil.

Set-up:

1. Set up a double boiler and follow the directions for candle making preparation.

2. Set out a mixing cup and a stirring stick for each child.

3. Cut a piece of foil for each child.

Procedure:

1. Melt the wax (about 2 ounces per child).

2. Color the wax yellow with the crayon.

3. Pour 2 ounces of the yellow wax into each cup.

4. Let the children stir the wax constantly until it becomes the consistency of clay. Remind them that the wax is still hot.

5. Have the children carefully take the wax out of the cups and form balls around a piece of wick. The ball should be about 2 inches across.

6. Flatten one side of the ball so that it will sit up. It will resemble an egg yoke.

7. Place the "yolk" on the piece of foil, making sure the wick is sticking straight out of the center of the yoke.

8. Fold up the edges of the foil, forming a circle around the yolk. Leave about 1 1/2 to 2 inches from the yolk to the edge of the foil.

9. Next melt some clear wax in a clean pot or can.

10. Let the clear wax cool for a few minutes and test it by pouring a small amount on the yolk making sure it does not start to melt.

11. Then carefully pour the clear wax around the yolk and let it harden.

12. When the wax has hardened, peel off the foil.

Root Beer Float Candles

Materials: Wax, a glass mug or soda fountain glass, a brown crayon, an old hand mixer, a double boiler, wicks, root beer scent (if you can find it at a candle or hobby store), pencils, and straws.

Set-up:

1. Set up a double boiler and follow the directions for candle making preparation.

2. Experiment with the wax to find out how much is needed to fill a mug or glass approximately 3/4 full, and then prepare enough wax to fill all the children's mugs or glasses.

Procedure:

1. Melt enough wax to fill each mug 3/4 full.

2. Color the wax with a brown crayon.

3. Drop in scent (optional).

4. Carefully pour the wax into the mug.

5. Tie the wick to the center of a pencil. Set the pencil horizontally across the mouth of the mug, so that the wick hangs down the center of the mug.

6. Insert the straw when the wax has started to form a film on top.

7. Let harden.

8. Next, melt the clear wax and let it cool for a few minutes.

9. Put the hand mixer into the melted wax and whip until the wax thickens, becomes white and looks like foam.

10. Remove the pencil, leaving the wick sticking straight up.

11. Top the root beer candle with the whipped wax. It will look like foam. Make sure the wick is sticking through the foam.

12. A cherry for the top can be made by molding warm red wax into a ball.

Comments: This project may be too expensive if you buy mugs or glasses for all the children. Check with local bars or restaurants for old mugs, or look for bargains at garage sales and variety stores. These make great presents and fundraisers!

Waxed Hands

Materials: Paraffin wax, a bag of ice, a bucket, crayon stubs, large coffee can, hot plate, a pan, an old large spoon, and a hot pad.

Set-up:

1. Set up a double boiler and follow the directions for candle making preparation.

2. Prepare a bucket of ice water about 2/3 full.

Procedure:

1. Fill the coffee can with wax chunks about 3/4 full.

2. Drop in several crayons to color the wax.

3. Put the can inside the double boiler pan and melt the wax, stirring occasionally.

4. When the wax has melted, carefully set the coffee can on the hot pad and let it cool somewhat.

5. Children's fingers must be slightly bent, but no fists.

6. Two children at a time can make wax hands by dipping their hands first into the ice water for a count of three and then dipping it into the melted wax for a count of three.

7. Continue until there is a wax buildup of 1/8" to 1/4."

8. Let the wax on their hands cool for 20 minutes. As the wax cools, it will expand.

9. Slowly pull the wax off the hand.

Comments: This project needs lots of supervision. Do not over-cook the wax. Younger children can do a wax finger instead of a hand.

Crayon Pressings

Materials: Old crayons, wax paper, an iron, cheese grater, or knife, scissors, hole punch and yarn.

Set-up:

1. Put pieces of wax paper down on the table.

2. Give each child a cheese grater or a knife for shaving. Give children instructions on how to use the grater or knives safely.

3. Peel the paper from the crayons.

4. Put the iron on a medium setting and assure proper supervision.

Procedure:

1. Let the children choose many crayons to shave.

2. Grate or shave the crayons onto the wax paper, leaving about 1" border around the sides.

3. Cover the crayon shavings with another piece of wax paper.

4. Have an adult or an older child, iron over the wax paper until the crayons melt.

5. When the pictures have cooled off, let the children cut the edges for decoration.

6. Punch a hole; string with yarn to hang in the window.

Comments: During autumn, add colorful leaves to the crayon shavings. Also pieces of construction paper, feathers and other decorations can be pressed in between the wax paper.

Sandpaper Crayon Transfer Pictures

Materials: Small pieces of coarse sandpaper, crayons, light-colored paper or cloth, and an iron.

Set-up:

1. Put the iron on a medium setting and assure proper supervision.

2. Put newspapers down on the surface of the ironing board or table.

3. Do a simple example with the children watching.

Procedure:

1. Draw a picture onto the sandpaper by making heavy marks with the crayons. Writing must be backwards to transfer correctly.

2. Put the sand paper, picture-side down, onto a piece of paper or cloth. The cloth must be about the size of the sand paper or bigger.

3. Cover with newspaper and iron evenly over the sand paper. The iron must be hot enough to melt the crayons.

4. After ironing, peel up a corner of the sandpaper to see if the picture is transferring; if not, keep going.

5. The picture will transfer from the sand paper onto the paper or cloth and take on the texture of the sand paper. The picture will still be left on the sand paper, so the children will have two copies to keep.

Comments: Make sure you use an old iron, because if wax gets on the iron it can be considered "dead" for ironing clothing.

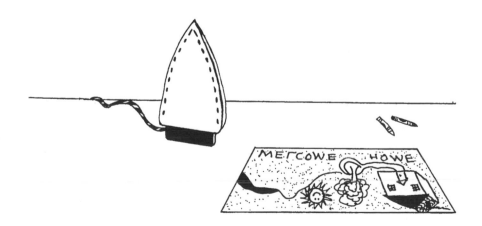

Melted Crayon Designs

Materials: Candles in holders, long crayons, newspapers, rubber bands, and construction paper.

Set-up:

1. This project needs very close adult supervision and is best done with older children.

2. Cover the table with newspaper; wax is difficult to remove.

3. Place one candle for every two children in the center of the table.

4. Peel off the paper from the crayons.

5. Put out construction paper and the peeled crayons.

Procedure:

1. Children simply hold the tip of the crayon in the flame of the candle for a few seconds until the crayon begins to drip.

2. Bring the crayon back over the paper and let the melted wax drip onto the paper, creating a design.

3. Change colors often.

Comments: Remember to put long hair into rubber bands and tie it back. Be sure there is plenty of adult supervision. Make sure the crayons are long enough not to burn any fingers.

More Crayon Melting

Materials: A warming tray or waffle iron, crayons, foil, and paper.

Set-up:

1. Plug in the warming tray or waffle iron.

2. Peel the paper off the top half of the crayons.

Procedure:

1. Put children's name on a waiting list.

2. Have children come up one at a time to the warming tray or waffle iron.

3. Draw a picture right onto the tray with the crayons, or place a piece of foil on the tray first and draw a picture on top of the foil.

4. Put a piece of paper over the tray (or foil) and press gently for a lift off.

Comments: Use an old warming tray as it will get very messy. The wax will wash off easily with hot water and cloth. For a similar effect, use the griddle side of a waffle iron. The waffle side can be used to make a rubbing-type melting project.

Recycling Crayons

Materials: Old crayon stubs, a muffin tin or other containers, and an oven.

Set-up:

1. Peel the paper off the crayon stubs.

2. Put out the muffin tin.

3. Pre-heat the oven at 400° for ten minutes.

Procedure:

1. Sort out the crayons into the muffin tins.

2. Mixing colors will create a rainbow crayon.

3. TURN OFF THE OVEN.

4. Put the muffin tin into the oven and let the crayons melt.

5. Let cool and the crayons will pop out. To speed up the cooling process, put the muffin tin in the freezer.

6. Children can draw pictures with the fat crayons.

Comments: The tins can be cleaned easily with hot water and soap. Try using metal chocolate molds as a variation.

Melted Crayon Swirl Pictures

Materials: A hot plate, crayon stubs, thin cardboard, a stick, metal spoon or nail, a shallow baking pan or cookie sheet, and a pair of pliers.

Set-up:

1. Heat water in the pan until hot (not boiling).

2. Peel off the paper from the crayon stubs.

3. Cut cardboard pieces or heavy paper that fit inside the pan.

Procedure:

1. Drop the crayon stubs into the water.

2. Let the colors melt.

3. Swirl the melted wax with a stick, spoon, or nail.

4. Next, take each piece of cardboard and fold back one corner.

5. Grasp the fold with the pliers and carefully dip the cardboard into the water. The crayon swirls will lift off the top of the water and onto the cardboard.

6. Let the cardboard dry on a clothes line.

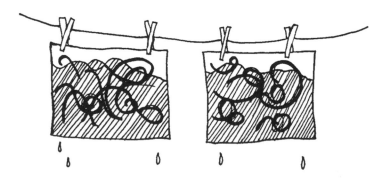

Three-Dimensional Art

There is a distinct developmental progression in children's work with materials that can be used three-dimensionally. The stages follow the same development as those in block building, from flat laid-out designs, to hesitant second story building, into full-fledged three dimensionability. Presenting materials and watching children create will tell a teacher a lot about each child's stage of growth. Allow room for differences.

Some Combinations of Materials

1. Soaked peas, or marshmallows, and toothpicks on a cardboard base.

2. Raisins and colored toothpicks on a foil-covered cardboard base.

3. Carrot slices and any of the above combinations. These can be done at snack time and then eaten.

4. Styrofoam packing materials or dough can be substituted for the food items.

5. Straws and paper clips. Bend the clips to form straight, corner, or angled joints. Pull the ends of the clips out to tighten the connections.

6. Paper cups and paper clips. Glue can be used to hold the mouth of the cups together; clips can be used for edges.

7. Small pieces of wood and glue.

8. Recycled aluminum cans, thin wire, and model cement.

9. Toothpicks and glue. Since building upward requires good small muscle coordination, this is recommended for older children. Fifth and sixth graders are capable of some very elaborate creations. The strongest building shape is the triangle; lots and lots of triangles are very sturdy when connected. For best results, the children should start with a flat base and build upward from it.

10. Tongue depressors and glue make great houses, bird feeders, boxes with lids, frames, and a variety of sculptures.

Aluminum Foil Figures

Materials: Aluminum foil and scissors.

Set-up: Cut varied sized rectangles from the foil.

Procedures:

1. Warn the children that the sharp edges of the foil can cause cuts.

2. Give children a rectangular-shaped piece of foil.

3. Have the children watch as the teacher does a step-by-step demonstration.

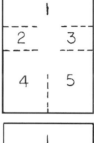

4. Cut the foil as shown (see diagram).

5. Crumble sections 2 and 3 first to form the arms. They should be crunched long and skinny (see diagram).

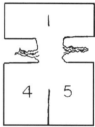

6. Crumble section 1 for the head. It should be pushed together into a ball. Do this carefully so the connection between head and arms does not rip. (This caution is the same for all remaining sections.)

7. Crumble section 4 and then 5 for the legs. Turn them up at the bottom for feet.

8. The last section to crumble is the body (it is the center part left over). Be extra gentle with this part.

9. Once all sections are crumbled and formed, the figure can be shaped into postures and motions. These can be anything appropriate that the children want to make; running, sitting, climbing, playing, etc. Animals can also be made out of these basic cuts; just turn them onto their feet.

Comments: This project produces a collection of strange and exotic creatures to line a shelf or display area. As a variation, have the children work together to create a farm or football team. It can also be used for storytelling and used with a moonscape or space theme. Finished products can also be painted.

Paper Roll Pictures

Materials: Thin strips of colored paper, scissors, paper glue, pencil, newspaper and regular construction paper (8 1/2" x 11".)

Set-up:

1. Cover the table with newspaper.

2. Place strips in long thin containers within reach of children.

3. Give each child a piece of construction paper for the base of the design.

Procedure:

1. Cut a strip to any desired length. Roll it over the pencil tightly.

2. Let it stay there for a minute, then slide the pencil out.

3. Glue the roll of paper onto the construction paper anywhere.

4. Do another strip the same way, varying the length and color.

5. In this way, cover the paper completely, in patterns, stacked up, etc. This project produces light, airy, colorful and interesting designs.

Newspaper Roll Geometric Structures

Materials: a large stack of newspapers, and rolls of masking tape.

Set-up:

1. This project should be done with grades 3-6, and can take several days to complete.

2. Explain to the children about polyhedrons (many faces) before starting this project, especially hexahedrons (six faces) and octahedrons (eight faces), three and four sided pyramids (tetrahedron and pentahedrons) and cubes. Familiarize them with the terms.

3. Showing a few examples is helpful. However, do not tell them this is a geometry project until after they have completed their structures.

4. Put the children into pairs or groups of four. Each group will make its own structure.

Procedure:

1. Put two sheets of newspaper together, flat on the table.

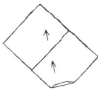

2. Roll them as tightly as possible, starting with one corner and rolling toward the diagonally opposite corner. This takes practice and patience, because the tighter the roll, the stronger the structure will be. Tape the corner edge in the center of the long roll to hold.

3. Make a large pile of these rolls.

4. Tape the ends of the rolls together in angles and shapes, starting with a basic flat shape. These can be triangles, squares, or any other shape the children decide to use. There should be a flap on each end of the rolls that is perfect for taping to another roll.

5. Add to the flat shape by building upward, or out.

6. Allow the children to create any type of shape they want.

7. When the group is finished, ask them to count the number of faces (open areas) and sides (newspaper rolls). The number of faces tells them the name of their shape.

8. The completed structures can be painted, or the faces covered with tissue paper and starch.

Hanging Animals or Objects

Materials: Very large paper or material (2 ft x 4 or 5 ft is good), staples, cotton or newspaper stuffing, marking pens, crayons, or fabric paint, and scissors.

Set-up: Decide on a theme for the animals or objects such as cactus plants, whales, dinosaurs, pumpkins, etc..

Procedure:

1. Draw large animals or shapes on the paper or fabric. For paper, cut out two of the pattern. For fabric, place the pattern on FOLDED material and cut it out.

2. Make certain that the sides fit together correctly.

3. Decorate one side of both pieces of the animal or object. (Let dry if fabric paints are used.)

4. Put the two sides together, and staple most of the way around the shape, leaving a section undone. (Sew, if using cloth.)

5. Stuff the shape with newspaper wads, cotton, shredded paper, or packing materials.

6. Finish stapling or sewing the sides together.

7. Use tape to reinforce the top in one or two sections. Punch a hole through the tape, and run a string or yarn through. Hang from the rafters or ceiling. If the shapes or animals are too big to hang, prop them up in corners or on chairs.

Comments: Fabric shapes can also be made smaller and used as pillows. Fabric glue is available in crafts shops.

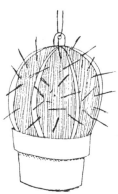

Yarn Mosaic Design Pictures

Materials: Colored balls of yarn, scissors, paper, newspapers, glue, and pencils.

Set-up:

1. Cover the table with newspaper.

2. Put out balls of yarn, scissors, pencils and paper for each child.

Procedure:

1. Have children draw a picture on the paper with a pencil. Remind them to make the picture simple with large spaces and little detail.

2. Using pieces of cut yarn, fill in the design or picture.

3. For older children, glue each piece of yarn down separately. For younger children, glue a small section of the picture and then press down pieces of yarn.

Comments: This is a time-consuming project. It can be worked on and finished over time. More complex designs will take longer to finish.

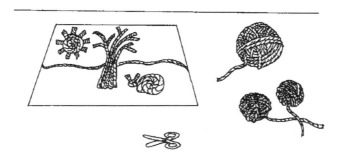

String Balloon Balls

Materials: Small balloons, string, liquid starch, white glue, containers to hold the balloons (baby food jar, yogurt container, margarine cup), and newspapers.

Set-up:

1. Cover the table with newspapers.

2. Mix liquid starch with glue (about four parts starch to one part glue) and put in a shallow dish.

3. Blow up the balloons and prop them on or slightly inside of containers.

4. Cut strings to workable lengths for children.

Procedure:

1. Soak the string in the starch/glue combination.

2. The children wind each string tightly around the balloon, leaving spaces in between. The smaller the spaces, the more sturdy the finished ball will be.

3. After the entire balloon is wrapped with string, let the ball dry over night.

4. Pop the balloon and pull it through an opening.

Comments: The string ball is fun for games of indoor catch. However, it is fragile. Yarn can also be used, but the starch/glue should be applied both by dipping and by using a paint brush. Yarn can be glued and coiled around the balloon without leaving a spaces. In this case the balloon will shrink inside after of few days of sitting.

Ojo de Dios — God's Eye

Materials: Two ice cream sticks or tongue blades, sticks, twigs or pencils; and colored yarn or string.

Set-up:

1. Have the children roll the yarn into balls. This is easier to work with than skeins of yarn which tangle easily.

Procedure:

1. Cross two equal-sized sticks in the middle.

2. Tie a knot with the yarn around the center of the sticks where they cross (see diagram).

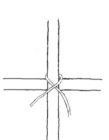

3. Weave the yarn over the top stick, around the underside, then over the stick again. Pull the yarn toward the next stick and repeat (see diagram).

4. Continue weaving around the crossed sticks, clockwise.

5. Change colors by tying the new color onto the old one.

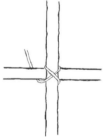

6. The ends can be decorated by hanging yarn pieces, tassles, feathers or beads.

Comments: Ojo de Dios means "eye of God" in Spanish. God's Eyes were often made as good luck pieces. Even the kindergarteners can do this project successfully. Try using other types of materials such as fibers, ropes, and rug yarn.

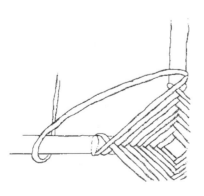

Balloon Piñata

Materials: A balloon, papier-mâché or liquid starch, toilet paper roll, newspapers, tissue paper, masking tape, paint, pencils, glue, candy or small toys.

Set-up:

1. Mix the papier-mâché paste (see recipes section) or use liquid starch.

2. Put newspapers down on the table.

3. Find a container to rest the balloon on while applying the papier-mâché.

Procedure:

1. Blow up the balloon and tie.

2. Tear the newspaper into small strips approximately 1" wide.

3. Moisten the newspaper strips with papier-mâché paste or starch, and wrap them smoothly around the balloon.

4. Cover the balloon so that no spaces are left, except for the tied end.

5. Let the balloon dry overnight; then put on one more coat of papier-mâché.

6. Twist a piece of newspaper into a rope to make a handle. Dunk the ends in papier-mâché paste or starch and lay each end on the top of the piñata and secure it with masking tape. Or reinforce the tie end of the balloon and when dry punch a hole in the reinforced area on each side. Run a sturdy string through to support piñata.

7. After it has dried completely, decorate the piñata with small squares of tissue paper; wrap squares around the eraser end of a pencil and stick with glue onto the piñata. Or cut tissue paper into strips that are about 4" wide; fold and cut to make frills or fringe. Paint may also be used.

8. When dry, pop the balloon; fill the piñata with candy/and or prizes, and close with tape.

9. Hang the handle from a rope and use as you would a regular piñata.

Comments: Start this project at least one week before your party day (unless you are in a very dry climate), because the piñata takes several days to dry. Make sure the handle is sturdy and firmly attached. Hang the piñata from a pole with a long string. As children wait in line, blindfold one child at a time and let them swing at the piñata with a bat or stick. Move the piñata up and down with the string, to make it more challenging for the older children. Make a rule that no one may jump and grab the treasure when it spills because this can cause injury. Have the children retrieve the treasure in small groups, each taking an equal amount of prizes.

Piñatas can be used for many holiday celebrations and also for themes such as dinosaurs and space. Large and small balloons and other items such as toilet paper and paper towel rolls and cardboard tubes can be put together to make animal shapes. For a really quick piñata, a cardboard box can be substituted for the balloon.

Bunny Baskets

Materials: 1/2 pint milk or orange juice cartons, construction paper, a marking pen, a hole punch, long pipe cleaners, sharp scissors, glue, and cotton balls.

Set-up:

1. Place the milk carton on its side and trace the bunny ears (see diagram).

2. Cut out the ears. Teachers and older children should cut out ears of each carton in advance.

3. Punch out two holes on either side of the head for the handle.

4. Make an example to show the children.

Procedure:

1. Glue the cotton balls onto the milk carton until it is covered completely (except the bottom).

2. Make eyes, whiskers, and inside of ears with construction paper and glue onto bunny basket.

3. Attach the pipe cleaners into the holes for the handle.

Paper Plate Rabbit

Materials: Two paper plates per child, scissors, stapler, pink, blue, and black construction paper, pipe cleaners, markers, cotton balls and glue.

Set-up:

1. Trace the ears and bow-tie on paper plates (see diagram).

2. Set out the materials on the art table.

3. Make a simple example.

Procedure:

1. Cut out the ears and bow tie from the paper plate and staple them to the other paper plate (rabbit head).

2. Cut out insides of the ears from pink construction paper.

3. Glue the insides of the ears in place.

4. Glue down cotton balls, covering the ears (except where pink is), and the head.

5. Cut eyes and whiskers from construction paper or use pipe cleaners for whiskers.

6. Decorate the bow tie.

7. Encourage the children to make the rabbits as individual as possible.

Native American Sand/Mud Painting

Materials: Sand, powered tempera paint, mud, cardboard, pencils, scissors, glue and paint brushes.

Set-up:

1. Mix about 2 cups of sand (white sand works best), cornmeal, or salt with 1/2 teaspoon of dry powered tempera paint to color.

2. Take the children on a nature walk to collect different types of soil. Let the mud dry out if wet.

3. Cut out cardboard pieces.

Procedure:

1. Draw a simple design on the cardboard with a pencil. Native American symbols make interesting designs. Fill in the design with glue.

2. Sprinkle colored sand or dried mud over glue.

3. Let dry.

Comments: There are several symbols that Native American use for religious purposes. It is not respectful to use these symbols in art projects. However, there are many symbols that are not religious. Children may want to make use symbols like the ones below, or design their own.

More Sand Painting

Materials: 25 lb. white sand, food coloring, rubbing alcohol, and large boxes.

Set-up:

1. Divide the sand into 5-6 equal parts, depending on how many colors you wish to use. Place each part into a separate box.

2. Mix 1/2 cup alcohol with about a 1 teaspoon of food coloring.

3. Add this mixture to a box of sand and stir thoroughly. This works best if it is done by hand, but the food coloring will stain hands.

4. Color each box of sand a different shade.

5. Allow them to dry completely. The alcohol will dry very quickly, especially if the sand is stirred occasionally.

6. The more food coloring used, the brighter the sand will become. Do NOT use water, it takes too long to dry.

Procedure: Same as preceding project.

Comments: This method using food coloring and alcohol instead of powered paint is preferred by some teachers because the dried sand is not as messy and is more permanent. However, the sand must dry completely first. The colors are more natural than using powdered paint.

Graham Cracker Houses

Materials: At least 4 whole graham crackers per child, eggs, powdered sugar, cardboard squares, foil, masking tape, and lots of types of candy and other sweets such as: red hearts, wafer cookies (doors), spice or gum drops, Life Savers, gummy bears and worms, mints, hard candies, pretzels (windows), M & M's, kisses, candy canes and peppermint sticks, marshmallows, chocolate chips, sprinkles, candied fruit slices, and small cookies.

Set-up:

1. Cut squares of cardboard and cover them with foil for bases. Put a piece of tape on one corner for names. Small houses should have at least 6 x 6 inch bases.

2. Younger children will need at least four whole crackers for a small house. Older children will want to make bigger houses and will need more crackers. Some houses can go into second and third stories!

3. Break eggs, separating the egg whites from yolks. Mix 4 egg whites with a pound of powdered sugar, until creamy. This amount will serve as the "glue" for approximately four houses, depending on their sizes.

4. Divide available candies into equal amounts per child and put aside until frame is dry.

Procedure:

1. For a small house, break all crackers in half.

2. Put a small amount of "glue" in the center of the foil base. Place one half of a cracker flat on the glue. This is the floor.

3. Dip all four sides of each cracker part into the "glue", and wipe off the excess. These are the walls and they are stood up along the side of the floor of the house. Balance them on each other for support and let them sit a while.

4. Dip another cracker piece in "glue" and place it flat on top of the sides to make the ceiling. Let this sit a while also.

5. For the roof. Dip opposite sides of two cracker halves into the glue and carefully place them on the ceiling to form the roof (see diagram). Let the whole house dry overnight.

6. The next day, have the children decorate the houses by dipping the candy pieces into the glue and placing them around the house and yard in interesting designs.

Comments: These houses are edible, and delightful to look at. Grown-ups love them! However, they are susceptible to ants, hungry siblings, pets, and sometimes parents. Don't wait too long to eat them.

Larger houses take more planning and teach a lot of architectural techniques. Children can create anything from California flat-roof houses with patios, to four story apartment buildings. When possible, let the parents help with the cost of making these.

Recipes

This section includes a variety of simple art recipes to make at school. It is a great way for children to learn about measurement, mixing ingredients, the cooking process, and how different art materials are made.

There are several homemade clay and dough recipes. To color or decorate, food coloring can be added to water when mixing the ingredients. This will make the whole batch of dough one color. Food coloring can also be added after the ingredients have been mixed but before they are kneaded. Take the amount of dough or clay desired, add a few drops of food coloring and knead. This allows for multi-colored clay.

After the clay or dough has either been dried or baked, paint can be used to decorate the objects. Acrylic paint works best. A clear gloss finish can be applied over the dried paint to add shine. Tempera paint can also be used. White glue mixed with tempera makes the paint glossier.

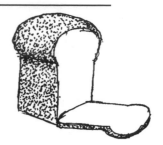

White Bread Clay

Ingredients:

- 8 slices of day old white bread
- 1/2 cup of white glue
- 1 tablespoon glycerin

How to make it:

1. Cut the crusts off the slices of white bread.

2. Crumble the bread into little pieces.

3. Place them in a bowl and mix them with the glue and glycerin.

4. Using your hands, mix the bread and glue together until they form a sticky clay-like blob.

5. Form a large ball of clay and take it out of the bowl.

6. Dust a clay board with flour before gently kneading the dough.

7. When it begins to get smoother, knead harder.

8. Continue kneading for about 5 minutes, until the clay is smooth and not very sticky.

9. Keep the clay wrapped tightly in plastic, when not in use, and store in the refrigerator.

10. The clay begins to harden very quickly when exposed to air. If this happens, add small drops of water to the dry dough.

11. After allowing the children to create objects, air dry the dough on wax paper for several days. Turn the objects over from time to time to prevent sticking and to let them dry evenly.

12. The clay can also be baked in an oven at 300° for 15 to 20 minutes. This will make the clay a brownish color.

13. When the clay is dry, it can be decorated.

Modeling Clay

Ingredients:

- 1 cup cornstarch
- 1 cup white flour
- a pinch of salt
- 2/3 cup water
- 1/2 cup cold water

How to make it:

1. Pour 2/3 cup water into a saucepan. Add salt.

2. Stir over medium heat for 4-5 minutes; then remove from heat.

3. Combine the cornstarch and the 1/2 cup cold water together. Add to the saucepan.

4. Stir the mixture together. Add flour. Stir until smooth.

5. Return saucepan to burner and cook until thickened.

6. Air dry the completed objects.

Baker's Dough

Ingredients:

- 4 cups white flour
- 1 cup salt
- 1 1/2 cups water

How to make it:

1. In a large bowl, combine flour and salt until well mixed.

2. Stir in 1 cup of water and continue to mix.

3. Slowly add the remaining water to the mixture as you turn the dough in the bowl.

4. Flour a working surface and knead the dough for ten minutes or more.

5. If the dough is too dry, wet your hand and continue kneading to moisten the dough. If dough is too wet, mix 1/4 cups of both salt and flour and sprinkle on the work surface and knead it into the dough. Continue to knead, allowing the salt and flour to mix into the dough.

6. Wrap the dough in plastic when you are not using it.

Baking instructions:

1. Bake the clay projects on a cookie sheet in a regular oven.

2. To prevent sticking, dust the cookie sheet with flour.

3. Bake at low heat 250 to 300°.

4. To check if the items are baked enough, let them cool slightly and press down gently. If they are pliable, they must be cooked longer. If they do not move when pressure is applied, they are done. The time will vary with the size and thickness of the dough. Begin by baking the items for 20 minutes and checking them. Check the larger items every 30 minutes.

5. Let the dough objects cool before decorating.

Goop - The Unusual But Amazing Substance!

Ingredients:

- 5 lbs. Salt
- 1 lb. cornstarch
- 4 C. Water
- Heat source
- Large pan
- Large bowl
- Large mixing spoon
- And a strong arm!

How to make it:

1. In a large pan add 5 lbs. salt and 2 cups water

2. Place over a medium heat and stir continuously and firmly

3. In a large bowl, blend 1lb. Cornstarch with 2 C. water, until it is a creamy solution.

4. Slowly add the cornstarch solution to the salt and water

5. Continue to mix in the pan over the medium heat.

6. Stir, stir, stir. Once this mixture is tougher to stir and begins to resemble mashed potatoes. You can either:

   - Continue to stir until it is thoroughly heated and blended,

   or

   - Dump it out onto a board or table when it begins to look like mashed potatoes. Knead it like bread dough until it is thoroughly mixed. It will be HOT, so be careful, use dishwashing gloves if you wish.

7. Roll the goop into tennis ball sized balls, cool and put in zip-loc baggies. Each batch will make about 12 balls, which will keep for several months. These balls can be shaped, and then painted with watercolor or tempera paints, immediately after shaping, or the following day. Watercolor sets are best.

8. Add food coloring to the water and cornstarch mixture early if you want specifically colored goop. (This is good for some projects, like geological layering).

9. Goop will stick to a cardboard surface for quite a while, and will last a long time once it is dried. Glue a tongue depressor to the backside of the cardboard to create a handle for carrying, or displaying these projects.

Uses for goop:

1. Landforms: Each child gets a ball of goop and a 5" x 5" (or larger) piece of cardboard. Shape the goop into a landform on the cardboard, and paint it with watercolors.

2. Volcanoes: Shape, paint, dry, then use vinegar (mixed with red food coloring) and baking soda in the central chamber. (Do the "exploding" part outside.) Volcanoes can be dried and used again a couple times.

3. Relief maps: Paint to match elevation.

4. Other type of maps: neighborhoods, countries

5. Create a nutritious model meal and paint it for display. Arrange it on a plastic plate.

6. Models of fruits and vegetables, including some that are halved to show the insides.

7. Skulls and skeletons for El Día De Los Muertos (Day of The Dead)

8. Faces, own or others

9. Hand prints

10. Fossils

11. Biology – internal organs, parts of things

12. Figurines/action figures

13. 3-D geometrical forms

14. Nature scenes

15. Holiday displays

16. Miniature dishes, pots and pans

Other ideas for incorporating Goop into the curriculum

1. Letter formation

2. Gifts for relatives

3. Plates and other dishes, cups

4. Layers for rock sedimentation - cut to show faulting, or push together for folding of mountains,

A note about Oobleck:

Oobleck = 1 box of cornstarch and about 1 1/2 C. water. Add food color to the mixture after you have made it smooth. There is a book called *Bartholomew and the Oobleck*, which is humorous to read with the Oobleck experience. Oobleck can dry out but it can be reanimated with water later. It dries on clothes and dusts off easily. NOT for constructing stuff…just fun. Scientifically this is neither a solid nor a liquid.

Glue Dough

Ingredients:

- 1/2 cup flour
- 1/2 cup white glue
- 1/2 cup cornstarch

How to make it:

1. Mix all the ingredients together in a bowl.

2. If the mixture is too dry, add glue; if it is too sticky, add flour.

3. Store the dough in a plastic tub while working with the dough.

4. The dough will air dry overnight.

Dough

Ingredients:

- 1 cup flour
- 1/3 cup salt
- 1/2 cup water
- A few drops of liquid detergent or vegetable oil

How to make it:

1. Combine flour and salt together in a large bowl.

2. Slowly add the water into the flour/salt mixture by stirring with a spoon.

3. If too dry, add a bit of water, and if too wet, sprinkle with flour; then knead.

4. When all ingredients have been mixed together, put down wax paper sprinkled with flour for the dough kneading.

5. The dough will harden in the air. When not in use, store in tightly closed plastic containers or bags. To keep for a week, store in refrigerator.

Cooked Dough

Ingredients:

- 2 cups baking soda
- 1 1/2 cups water
- 1 cup cornstarch

How to make it:

1. Combine ingredients in a large bowl.

2. Add food coloring to the water for color.

3. Mix with a fork until the mixture is smooth.

4. Place in a pot and boil over moderate heat until it thickens.

5. Let cool and spoon onto wax paper.

Soap Dough

Ingredients:

- 1/2 cup liquid starch
- 4 tablespoons salt
- 1 cup liquid soap
- 1/8 cup water
- 2 cups cornmeal

How to make it:

1. Mix the food coloring with the liquid starch for color.

2. Combine all the materials in a large bowl.

3. Put out pieces of wax paper.

4. Give each child a ball of soap dough.

5. Let the dough creations air dry.

Natural Dough

Ingredients:

- 1 cup flour
- 1 cup water
- 1/2 cup salt
- 2 tablespoons vegetable oil
- 2 tablespoons cream of tartar (optional)
- Beet, spinach or carrot juice for coloring

How to make it:

1. Combine the salt, flour and oil together in a large mixing bowl.

2. Slowly add the water.

3. Cook over medium heat.

4. Stir the mixture until the dough becomes stiff.

5. When cooled, knead the dough until it feels smooth.

6. Add a few drops of the vegetable juices for coloring. The beet juice will make pink dough, the spinach juice, green dough, and the carrot juice, orange-yellow dough.

7. Store the dough in tightly closed plastic containers or bags in the refrigerator.

Chinese Style Dough

Ingredients:

- 3 1/2 cups white flour
- 1 1/2 cups sweet rice flour
  (also known as glutinous rice flour;
  purchase at Asian food stores)
- 7 teaspoons salt
- 4 teaspoons honey
- 1 3/4 cup water

How to make it:

1. Combine both types of flour and salt in a large mixing bowl.

2. Boil the water and add 1 1/2 cups to the flour and salt mixture.

3. Slowly add 1/4 to 1/2 cups more boiling water. The mixture should be dry; it should bind together but not be sticky.

4. Form the dough into a flat lump. Steam for 30 minutes in a double boiler.

5. When steamed, break into small lumps and cool on a rack or on a towel.

6. When cooled, knead in 4 teaspoons of honey, a bit at a time.

7. Color by adding a few drops of food coloring or powered tempera paint when kneading.

8. Knead into dough. Keep wrapped tightly in a plastic bag or covered with a damp towel.

9. This clay retains it shape without shrinking, and air-dries into strong, hard clay. It can be used to make delicate projects. Artists in China use this dough to make colorful clay figures.

Oil-like Paint

Ingredients:

- Powdered tempera paint or "Biggy" cake paints (one part)
- Liquid dishwashing detergent (two parts).

How to make it:

1. Mix the paint and detergent together until it makes a very thick and creamy paint.

2. Use a Popsicle stick to spread the paint onto paper.

3. Paint in layers to look like real oil paint.

Quick Fingerpaint Recipe

Ingredients:

- 1 cup liquid starch
- 1 cup liquid tempera paint
- 1 or 2 spoonfuls of powdered soap or liquid soap

How to make it:

1. In a shallow paint container, mix the above ingredients until smooth.

2. Spoon onto finger paint paper, shelf paper, or directly onto the table.

Another Quick Fingerpaint Recipe

Ingredients:

- Wallpaper paste or wheat paste
- Tempera paint
- Lukewarm water

How to make it:

1. Mix the wallpaper paste with lukewarm water until smooth.

2. Keep mixing and adding the paste until you have the desired thickness.

3. Add the tempera paint and mix.

Cooked Fingerpaint

Ingredients:

- 1 cup cornstarch
- 2 cups of cold water
- 2 envelopes unflavored gelatin
- 1 cup powdered soap

How to make it:

1. Dissolve the cornstarch in 1 1/2 cups of cold water.

2. Soak the gelatin in the remaining 1/2 cup of cold water.

3. Combine the two.

4. Cook over medium heat, stirring from time to time. The paint should become thick and glossy.

5. Mix in the soap and stir well.

6. Add powdered paint, or a few drops of food coloring, and store in jars with lids.

More Cooked Fingerpaint

Ingredients:

- 1 1/2 cups laundry starch
- 1/2 cup talcum powder
- Food coloring or tempera paint
- 4 cups boiling water
- 1/2 cup powdered soap

How to make it:

1. Mix the starch with cold water until it is thick and creamy.

2. Add the boiling water to the mixture, stirring constantly until it becomes transparent.

3. Cook the mixture. Add 1/2 cup soap flakes and 1/2 cup talcum powder. Stir until they are well mixed.

4. Add tempera paint or food coloring.

5. Beat with an eggbeater until the paint is smooth and thick.

6. Store in the refrigerator in plastic containers.

Papier-Mâché Paste

Ingredients:

- 1 cup non-rising wheat flour
- 1/4 cup sugar
- 1 quart warm water

How to make it:

1. Mix together flour and sugar in a saucepan.

2. Stir in a small amount of warm water.

3. Stir constantly and bring to a boil.

4. Cook until it is thick and clear.

5. Use when warm for best results. Tear small strips of newspaper and dip into paste mixture for papier-mâché projects.

6. Wallpaper paste (follow the directions on the box) or liquid starch one part starch mixed with 1/2 parts glue, both make good papier-mâché mixtures.

Chalk

Ingredients:

- 2 tablespoons of powdered tempera paint
- 1/2 cup water
- 3 tablespoons of plaster of Paris
- Small paper cups

How to make it:

1. Mix all ingredients together.
2. Pour into a paper cup.
3. Let harden for an hour or so.
4. Peel away the cup.

Paste

Ingredients:

- 1/2 cup water
- 1 cup flour

How to make it:

Mix the two ingredients together in a bowl.

Wheat Paste

Ingredients:

- 1 1/2 cups boiling water
- 2 teaspoons wheat flour
- 1/2 teaspoon salt

How to make it:

Mix the ingredients together and store in a plastic or glass jar with a lid.

Nature Crafts

The great outdoors is a wonderful place to collect items for crafts projects. By using natural items, children learn about the world around them. Many children enjoy going on neighborhood walks or field trips to collect these materials. It is important to teach children to be respectful of nature; pick wild flowers only where they grow abundantly. Never take more than 10% of a clump or pull them up by their roots. Tread gently so the ecology is not disrupted and leave an are as neat as you found it. Take cones, twigs, pods, and leaves from the ground whenever possible, rather than pulling them off the trees. Never pull whole branches or stalks off of plants or trees. Pinch leaves off gently and take from a wide range of the plant rather than just off one branch. Be sure to teach children why it is important to be respectful of nature.

Several of the nature crafts projects involve using food such as fruits, vegetables and seeds. Some people feel that the use of food is inappropriate for crafts project because there is so much hunger in the world. Please use your own judgment and discretion.

Sand Casting with Plaster

Materials: Plaster of Paris, a coffee can, damp sand, rocks, shells, drift wood, beach glass, and other interestingly shaped objects.

Set-up:

1. This project can be done at the beach or at the program site. If at the program, put wet sand in a shallow box. If at the beach, the mold can be made right in the sand.

2. Collect the rocks, shells and other items.

Procedure:

1. Make a mold by scooping out the wet sand. Leave at least two inches of sand covering the bottom of the box. For a fish shape make the mold 6 inches wide, 12 inches long and 2 inches deep. For a fossil the mold can be round in shape. other possibilities include: an impression of a shell, a child's hand or foot, or a free-form pattern.

2. Press the shells, rocks and other found items into the bottom of the mold. Holes can be poked into the sand for indentations.

3. Mix the plaster in the coffee can according to the directions on the box.

4. Stir the plaster with hands or an old long spoon.

5. Wait five minutes and then pour the plaster carefully into the mold.

6. Let the sand cast harden for at least one hour and lift it out of the sand.

7. Brush off the loose sand.

Comments: Plaster of Paris should not be poured down a drain and can not be washed out of containers. It hardens very quickly, so do not mix it in advance.

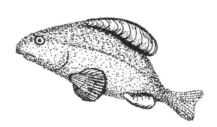

Painted Rocks

Materials: Rocks of all shapes and sizes (smooth ones and round ones work best), acrylic paints, glue, yarn, shells, wiggle eyes, pipe cleaners, cardboard, and felt.

Set-up:

1. Collect rocks and pebbles.

2. Clean and dry the rocks before painting.

3. Cut cardboard bases for the rock creations if desired.

Procedure:

1. Children glue rocks together to create dolls, people, animals, monsters, etc. They may also glue rocks together to make free-form rock sculptures.

2. Glue smaller rocks onto the larger ones for the head, arms, and legs.

3. Paint faces, clothing, designs, etc.

4. Yarn and felt can be added for hair and clothing. Wiggle eyes and pipe cleaners can be used to create bugs or monsters.

5. Small shells can be glued on for decoration.

Comments: Shoe boxes, egg cartons or other containers can be decorated to hold or display the painted rocks.

Driftwood Sculpture

Materials: Driftwood pieces, small shells and rocks, glue.

Set-up:

1. Collect the driftwood pieces, shells and rocks.

2. Ask the children to find the most interesting pieces of driftwood they can.

Procedure:

1. Children put pieces of driftwood together to create sculptures. They can make animals, people or free form shapes.

2. Glue on shells, rocks or any other object needed to achieve the effect.

Comments: Driftwood, shells and small rock can also be made into mobiles. Use twigs with string to support the nature items.

Leaf Decorations on Cards and Stationery

Materials: Colorful leaves (of all shapes, sizes and varieties), newspaper, glue and heavy weight paper, large index cards or cardboard.

Set-up: Collect leaves with the children.

Procedure:

1. Press the leaves between pieces of newspaper by placing a heavy book or object on top of them until they dry. This will take several days.

2. For stationery, cut paper into several pieces of the same size.

3. Carefully glue a leaf or some leaves on the top of the paper. Or glue onto light cardboard or index cards to make greeting cards.

Flower Painting

Materials: Colorful flowers and weeds, paper.

Set-up: Collect flowers or weeds in your neighborhood such as dandelions, goldenrod, wild aster and/or any other colorful flowering plant. Also ask your local floral shop to donate old flowers such as roses, carnations, etc.

Procedure:

1. Children use the flower heads and rub them on the paper.

2. For large flowers, several petals can be rolled into a ball and then rubbed onto paper. The color pigment of the flowers will transfer onto the paper.

Comments: Younger children will be fascinated by seeing the color pigment transfer onto the paper. For older children it is a good comparison study of different flower colors.

Natural Paints

Materials: A variety of items such as parsley, black tea, grape skins, red cabbage, beets, pear leaves, cherry leaves, blueberries, flower petals, oak bark, and green leaves, a sauce pan, a burner, water, paint brushes, light colored paper and containers for paint.

Set-up:

1. Collect the plants and items that will be used for the paint.

2. Show the children examples of natural dyes.

Procedures:

1. Separately chop or shred small pieces of the plant materials.

2. Put plant materials in a sauce pan one at a time with a very small amount of water (just enough to prevent burning) and simmer until the water turns colorful.

3. Pour the colored water into paint containers and let cool.

4. Paint on a light colored paper with brushes.

Painting with Nature

Materials: Paper: Large containers for paint, paint, a choice of corn cobs with or without corn, a pineapple, pine needle clusters, a pine cone, cattails, leafy tops of vegetables such as beets, celery, parsnips, radishes, turnip or carrots that will be used as "paint brushes."

Set-up:

1. Collect the items that will be used for painting.

2. Set out paint in shallow dishes and paper.

Procedure:

1. Dip the "brushes" into paint and paint with them.

2. Corncobs, pineapples (cut off the leaves) and pine cones should be rolled into paint and evenly coated, then rolled across the paper.

Air Drying Flowers

Materials: Flowers, a wire coat hanger, rubber bands, string, long pipe cleaners, a shoe box, a nail, and waterproofing spray.

Set-up:

1. Pick the flowers on a sunny day when they are in full bloom and make sure they are not wet with dew. The best time to pick flowers is in the morning.

2. Cut the stems as long as possible and on a slant.

Procedure:

1. To prepare the flowers for drying, pull all the leaves off the stem.

2. Bunch the flowers together, put only three together if the flower is large; put up to six together for smaller flowers.

3. Twist one end of a long pipe cleaner tightly around the stems of a bunch of flowers.

4. Twist the other end of the pipe cleaner over the wire rod of the hanger and hang four to six bunches of flowers upside-down (see diagram).

5. Suspend the hangers in a warm, dry, dark room, garage or basement.

6. Let dry two to three weeks (the larger the flower, the longer it will take to dry. The stems will shrink and become stiff.

7. To preserve the flowers, spray with waterproofing spray.

Comments: Dried flowers can be used for a variety of crafts projects. They look beautiful in homemade vases, wall hangings, weaving, and baskets. Carpentry projects can be enhanced with dried flowers. Seed pods and natural materials such as berries can also be air-dried. Some flowers will wilt and shrink when air-dried. There are books listing which flowers work best, or you can experiment with many flowers to see which work well.

Old-Fashioned Flower Pressing

Materials: Small flat flowers such as pansy, phlox or primrose, ink blotter or smooth paper towel, and heavy books (dictionary or big city telephone book).

Set-up:

1. Pick the flowers on a hot sunny day and make sure they are dry. Check if there are areas where flower picking is permitted or prohibited. Also ask neighborhood garden owners if some flowers can be picked. If there is no place to pick fresh flowers, purchase them.

2. Cut off the stems at the base of the flower; save some for pressing.

3. The flowers can be picked at different stages of growth.

Procedure:

1. Open each of the books about 1/2 inch from the back cover. Lay the blotter or paper towel on the right side of the page (see diagram).

2. Place freshly picked flowers face down on the blotter and press down the center of the flower with your index finger.

3. When the blotter is filled with flowers, cover it with another blotter or paper towel. For additional flowers, turn down another 1/2 inch thickness of pages and press the flowers as above.

4. Close the book when all the flowers are in between the pages. To press the flowers, put several heavy books on top of the book with the flowers inside.

5. Place in a dry, warm place and let sit for at least two weeks.

6. Dried flowers will have hard stiff centers and petals that feel brittle.

Modern Flower Pressing

Materials: Flowers, silica gel (sodium silicate which can be purchased from a drugstore, flower shop or craft shop), a large box and large plastic bag.

Set-up:

1. See **Old-Fashioned Flower Pressing** for picking and preparation of flowers.

2. Cut two pieces of blotter paper to fit inside of the box.

Procedure:

1. Place one piece of blotter paper in the box and cover with 1/4 inch silica gel. The gel preserves the flowers natural color and absorbs wetness.

2. Put the flowers on top of the silica gel in a single layer leaving space between the flowers.

3. Cover the flowers with another 1/4 inch layer of silica gel and then cover with a second piece of blotter paper.

4. Put a heavy book on top of the box; then carefully place the box with the book into a plastic bag. Tightly close the bag.

5. Place several more books on top of the plastic bag.

6. Keep on a level surface in a dry, warm room.

7. Let dry two to three days.

Comments: If the petals are not smooth, place the flowers back inside a book for a few more days without the blotter of gel. Pressed flowers make wonderful crafts projects. They can be glued onto paper for stationery, pressed into clay, or used to make pictures and decorate windows.

Old-Fashioned Vegetable Egg Dyeing

Materials: Eggs, cheesecloth or clean old nylons, a twist tie, vinegar, scissors, a small pan, a burner and the following materials for dyes: *Blue:* red cabbage leaves or blueberries; *Pink:* rose hips, cherries or pickled beet juice; *Bluish purple:* diced beets; *Pale green:* spinach leaves, young grass, broccoli, or carrot tops; *Bright yellow:* saffron tea; *Pale yellow:* yellow onion skins, dandelions, or goldenrod flowers; *Dark brown:* red and brown onion skins; *Light brown:* walnut shells; *Brown:* coffee or tea; *Purple:* grape juice; *Orange:* grated carrots

Set-up:

1. Purchase or collect the materials for they dye colors you want.

2. Cut the cheesecloth or nylons into 4" x 4" pieces.

Procedure:

1. Chop a vegetable up into small pieces.

2. Put 3 tbs. of the chopped vegetables in the center of the cheesecloth.

3. Center the egg in piece of cheesecloth and spread the vegetable chunks around it evenly.

4. Secure the cheesecloth around the egg with a twist tie.

5. Place the wrapped egg in a small pan, cover with water so there is about 1/2" of water over the egg.

6. Bring to a boil and simmer for about ten minutes.

7. Let the egg cool in the water.

8. Add one teaspoon of vinegar.

Comments: This is a long process, and you will need new water and vinegar for each egg and color. This project produces eggs with patterns around them. The eggs can be eaten after the dyeing process.

Natural Egg Dyeing

Materials: Hard boiled, raw or blown eggs, salt (raw eggs only), vinegar, a pot, and a burner. Use the same materials for dyes as found in **Old-Fashioned Vegetable Egg Dyeing**.

Set-Up: Simmer all ingredients separately, except the pickled beet juice and the grape juice.

Procedure:

1. Talk to the children about the use of natural dyes in clothing, painting, pottery, and art pieces.

2. Dye some eggs and see if the children can guess what materials were used to make the color.

3. Simmer eggs with one of the ingredients mentioned above.

4. For the pink dye, soak hard-boiled eggs in pickled beet juice

5. To dye the eggs a lavender shade, soak them in grape juice.

6. If raw eggs are used, put several into a pan with a pinch of salt. Add a large handful of dyeing materials and bring to a boil. Immediately reduce the heat and simmer the eggs for 12 minutes. This method produces a richer, brighter dye color. Cool with 1 tsp. vinegar added to water before removing.

Comments: This project produces solid colored eggs. Dyeing eggs naturally is very educational. However, it is time consuming. The easiest way to color eggs is with commercial food coloring (liquid or tables). White crayons drawn on the eggs before dyeing will result in a resist-type design. Other colored crayons can be used to create patterns between the dye. Eggs can be dipped into more than one color. Hand painting eggs is also a fun activity. Another variation is wrapping yarn around eggs. The eggs can be eaten after the dyeing process.

Oak Leaf Egg Dyeing

Materials: Fresh oak leaves, eggs, rubber band or string, a pot and burner.

Set-up:

1. Collect fresh oak leaves.

2. Hard boil the eggs.

3. Set the leaves and other materials on the art table.

Procedure:

1. Wrap oak leaves around an egg and fasten securely with rubber bands or string.

2. Simmer several eggs for seven to ten minutes.

3. Remove the eggs from the pot and let cool.

4. Gently peel the leaves off. The leaves will make a dapple brownish effect on the eggs.

Comments: The eggs can be eaten after they have been dyed.

Seed Decorating

Materials: Seeds of all shapes, colors, sizes and textures, varnish (optional), glue, and items to be decorated with seeds, such as burlap, corkboard, felt, a blown egg, cardboard, a glass jar, a tin, and plastic containers.

Set-up: Collect or purchase seeds. Have children bring in dried fruit and vegetable seeds. On nature walks collect flower heads, fir cones, acorns, sycamore ad ash wings and other seeds. Corn and other seeds can be purchased at pet shops. Look for wheat, maple, sesame seeds, peas, sunflower seeds, bird food, gold sweet corn, black-eyed peas, millet, Chinese and European lentils, brown, red, white, soya, pale green flageolet, and black beans at local grocery stores, international food and health food shops.

Procedure:

1. Seeds can be used to decorate a variety of items. For a simple design, have children draw a picture on cardboard, glue and fill it in with seeds. For a more complex project, seeds can be used to decorate bottles, cardboard boxes, jars, and cans. Wall hangings can be made on cloth, burlap, and felt. Use a strong piece of cardboard for the backing and frames. Corkboard and wooden panels can be decorated with seeds without any backing. Blown eggshells can be decorated with seeds and hung from a tree or window.

2. To glue the seeds, it is best to begin with a simple design using middle-sized and larger seeds. younger children should put the glue down first and then carefully place each seed on top of the blue. Older children may use a toothpick or small paintbrush to apply the glue to the back of each seed. Smaller seeds create more elaborate design but are difficult to use. Shells can be including the design for variation.

3. Let the seeds dry before applying varnish. Glue mixed with water can also be applied. The varnish will increase the richness of the color and will protect the seeds from dust. It also will help keep the small seeds in place. If the design is made on fabric or glass, the varnish must be brushed on very carefully to avoid touching the background. Spray varnish can also be used on painted backgrounds.

Planting & Growing

Spring is a fabulous time to do planting and growing activities with children. If you are fortunate enough to have an outside garden, children can learn the process of plant growth first hand. Even if you do not have an outside garden, there are many different gardening projects you can do. Everything from growing mold to planting indoor bulbs to caring for hanging plants provides children with interesting hands-on experiences with plant life. Allowing the children to take responsibility for the proper care of the plants enhances their experiences.

Ideas for Planting and Growing Projects

Fruits and Vegetable Gardens

Try growing:

avocado pits, potatoes, pineapple tops, carrot tops, fruit seeds, bulbs, pop corn kernels, peanuts, beans

Planting and Growing Experiments

Try science experiments when introducing planting and growing:

1.Purchase three identical plants. Put one in a very sunny place, one in a partly sunny place and place one in the shade. Care for each plant the same. Have children note the progress of each plant.

2.Plant several of the same seeds in different types of soil. See which one is the most healthy and thriving.

3.Purchase different types of plant food and see which is most effective.

4.Try a variety of ways to sprout seeds such as cotton balls sitting in jars with water, in soil, and in jars of water. Which works best?

Potato Creatures

Materials: Potatoes, potting soil, grass seeds, a knife, a spoon, marking pens, tooth picks; for decorations: raisins, small marshmallows, buttons, material, etc.

Set-up:

1. Bring in potatoes with no sprouted eyes.

2. Make sure you have a sunny window sill or table on which to place the potatoes.

Procedure:

1. Cut the potatoes in half either lengthwise or vertically.

2. Scoop out the insides of the potatoes.

3. Fill the insides with potting soil.

4. Plant the grass seeds inside.

5. Use tooth picks for legs.

6. Draw a face on the potato with a marking pen and decorate.

7. Small pieces of potato can be cut for ears and tails and secured with tooth picks.

8. Put in a sunny place and keep moist.

Comments: Monsters, bunnies, cats, people, and other creatures can be created. Send them home as soon as the grass has grown a few inches because the potatoes will start to rot after a week or so. Some people feel that the use of food is inappropriate for crafts projects because there is so much hunger in the world. Please use your own judgment and discretion. Other containers can be substituted for the potatoes such as egg cartons, milk cartons, or margarine tubs.

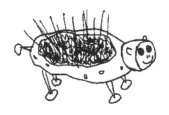

Mini Gardens

Materials: A variety of seeds in packages, egg cartons, potting soil, small rocks, tooth picks, paper clips, and masking tape.

Set-up:

1. This project is best done outdoors, or with newspaper covering the art table.

2. Open the seed packages, making sure not to rip the name of the seed.

3. Put out the above materials for each child.

Procedure:

1. Sprinkle a small layer of rocks into each cup of the egg carton, for drainage.

2. Fill each egg cup 3/4 full with potting soil.

3. Push fingers into the soil to make holes for the seeds.

4. Plant two or three seeds in each of the twelve egg cups (follow the directions on each package), and cover with soil.

5. Label the seeds by making mini-signs (masking tape folded over a tooth pick).

6. Bring the gardens indoors, put them in a sunny place, and water them daily.

Comments: Plastic plant containers with holes in the bottom also work well for mini gardens. Plants can be replanted in gardens or large pots.

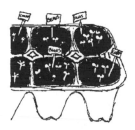

Hairy Sponges

Materials: Sponges, a marking pen, sharp scissors, fast growing seeds such as grass, a pie tin or shallow dish, and plenty of sunshine.

Set-up: Make sure you have a window sill or table that receives ample sunlight.

Procedure:

1. Draw a shape or object on the sponge.

2. Cut out the shape.

3. Wet the sponge shape.

4. Place the sponge shape in the shallow dish of water.

5. Press the seeds into the holes of the sponge.

6. Put in a sunny place.

7. Keep moist.

Comments: The seeds will grow out of the sponge shape. This is a great project for St. Patrick's Day. Cut the sponges into shamrocks and plant grass seeds. Pop-up sponge sheets can be purchased that expand when placed in water. (See Sponge Painting in the Painting Section for more information).

Hanging Sponge Gardens

Materials: small sponges, clear plastic bags, fast growing seeds (grass, clover, mustard, chia or herbs), and strings.

Set-up: The gardens need to be suspended in a sunny spot.

Procedure:

1. Moisten the sponges.

2. Push the seeds into the holes of the top side of the sponge.

3. Carefully place the sponge inside a plastic bag with the seeds facing upwards.

4. Tie the string around the top of the bag and suspend in a sunny spot.

5. Watch the seeds germinate inside the bag!

6. Keep moist. They can be transplanted but many will not survive.

Sprouts

Materials: Alfalfa seeds, mung beans, lentils, soy beans or other edible legumes and seeds; small clean window screen(s) covered with light weight porous fabric (i.e. muslin, gauze); jar(s) to soak seeds, area to drain the screen easily.

Set-up:

1. If a regular window screen is available, just measure and cut the fabric to fit on it, and another piece to go over the top so light does not get directly on the screen.

2. Screens can be made with hardware store screening material, wooden frames and staples and small nails.

3. Test the fabric to make sure water will drain through it easily, before using it on the screens.

Procedure:

1. Soak a handful of the seeds or beans in the jar for several hours, up to eight, but not longer. How many seeds used will depend on the size of the screen and the type of seeds or bean. The seeds will need to have room to grow.

2. Drain the water from the seeds or beans, and spread them out evenly on the fabric covering the screen. Put another layer of the fabric over the seeds or beans. Set in a shady spot that is not too cold.

3. For the next few days, water the seeds on the screen twice a day. This is done by lightly spraying water over the seeds directly, and allowing the water to drain off immediately. (Doing this over lawn or some other water loving vegetation is best to conserve water use). Re-cover the seeds each time they are watered.

4. Make sure that the seeds do not sit in any water while on the screen, and if the watering process causes them to clump together, lightly spread them out again by hand.

5. After three or four days, the seeds or beans will be ready to harvest. Legumes will take longer than smaller seeds, alfalfa is the fastest growing. Uncover the tray and expose the sprouts to sunlight for several hours, 4 to 12. The leaves will turn green.

6. Now eat them for snack. Try different types for a taste experience. Cooking the legume sprouts is also a taste treat mixed with rice or noodles. Wheat sprouts are very sweet and can be added to bread, however, they should be harvested without the sunlight exposure.

Comments: Purchasing some sprouts at the grocery store will show children what they can expect to see, and also give the teacher an idea of what the seeds and beans should look like when they are ready. Seeds will grow at different rates depending on type, temperature and light around them, and amounts of water. Drainage is very important. If the weather is very warm, water the seeds a third time each day. Adults should try the whole cycle in advance at home, to insure that the seeds are viable, the soaking time works, and to determine how long each type of seed takes in their climate.

Indoor & Outdoor Games

Games are a very important part of childhood. Children learn both cooperation and competition through a variety of games in which they participate. Games are best taught with a spirit of fun and sharing rather than competition for winners and losers. Many children play intensely competitive team sports in leagues. The games at an after school program focus attention on skill development, posture, group interaction and willingness to include children who may be less "athletic."

There are many traditional games such as the different forms of tag, four square, dodge ball, jump rope, baseball, and kickball. These games are usually organized and initiated by the children themselves. Certain games are often popular for a length of time, then other games replace them. The following are games which may be adult-initiated. Some are better suited for indoors; others more for outdoors, and some it does not make a difference. Many use nonverbal communication, an important skill for children to learn.

Mouse Trap   For Grades K-2

Setting: Outdoors or a large indoor space.

Materials: None

Set-up: 9 to 12 children are needed, a larger group can also play.

Procedure:

1. Choose five to six children to join hands and make a circle. They are the "trap."

2. Choose one player to be the cat and the remaining players to be mice.

3. The "trap" opens and closes by having the children raise and lower their hands. When their hands are raised the trap is open, when their arms are down, the trap is closed.

4. The cat must turn his or her back and count to twenty, while the children who make up the trap open and close the trap.

5. During this time the mice scamper in and out of the trap, being careful not to get caught inside the trap.

6. After counting, the cat quickly turns around and yells "SNAP!"

7. The children who make up the trap quickly close the trap. All the mice caught inside the trap become part of the trap.

8. This process continues until the last mouse is left. He or she then becomes the cat.

Wiggle Waggle, Catch the Tail   For All Grades

Setting: Outdoors

Materials: None

Set-up: A minimum of six players, the more the better.

Procedure:

1. Players form a line, each player holding the waist of the person in front.

2. The front person is the "head" and the last person is the "tail."

3. The "head" tries to catch the "tail" of the line.

4. The children in line must stay holding the waist of the person in front of them (the animal must stay intact).

5. Once the animal breaks apart, the game is stopped and started over.

6. When the "tail" is tagged by the "head," the next person in line becomes the "head" and the former "head" goes to the back, to become the "tail."

Hook Up Tag   For Grades 2-6

Setting: Outdoors or a large indoor space.

Materials: None

Set-up: Ten or more players are needed (an even number of players if possible).

Procedure:

1. One player is selected to be "it" and one player is selected to be chased.

2. The other players find a partner and link arms.

3. The linked pairs arrange themselves in a circle with the "it" player in the middle and the player to be chased on the outside of the circle.

4. The "it" player says "GO" and starts to chase the player on the outside of the circle.

5. The player being chased links up with a pair. At this time he or she yells "GO" and the person on the other end of the pair must detach and run, trying to find another pair to link up with.

6. The "it" player is always trying to tag any player who is not linked up with a pair.

7. When tagged, the person switches places with "it" and begins chasing the other player.

Comments: The players in pairs must remain in a circle as well as they can.

Streets and Alleys   For Grades 2-6

Setting: Outdoors or large indoor space.

Materials: None

Set-up: This game is best played with a large group, at least 20.

Procedure:

1. Choose one child to be the "Cat" and another to be the "Mouse."

2. Have the remaining children stand in even rows of four children or more holding hands and facing forward.

3. Explain that when they are holding hands and facing forward they are in STREET formation. Thus the children make horizontal rows.

4. To make the ALLEYS, they must turn sideways and hold hands with the child in front of and behind them. Thus the children make vertical rows.

5. The game leaders repeatedly call "Streets" and "Alleys" until the children understand what to do and can change quickly.

6. To begin the game the cat starts inside the front street and the mouse stands inside the back street.

7. The teachers calls "begin" and the cat chases the mouse. Both the cat and mouse must stay inside the streets.

8. After a minute or so, the teacher calls "Alleys," and the children quickly form alleyways. Again the cat and mouse must stay within the alleys.

9. This continues until the cat tags the mouse. At this time two new players are chosen to be cat and mouse.

Comments: The words cat and mouse can be changed to anything as long as one clearly chases the other.

Rock/Scissors/Paper   For Grades 1-6

Setting: A large space is necessary for this game and it can be played both indoors or out.

Materials: Chalk or tape to make a center line.

Set-up: Two teams are needed.

1. Each team must have a "free zone" designated at opposite ends of the playing area.

2. A center line must be made dividing the two teams.

Procedure:

1. Divide the children into two teams. Show them where their "free zone" is located.

2. Each team huddles collectively and decides which symbol they are going to show (rock/scissors/paper).

3. Rock breaks scissors, paper covers rock and scissors cut paper.

4. Once the teams have decided on a sign, they meet at the center line and face each other.

5. At the count of 1-2-3, each team shows their sign.

6. The team that shows the winning symbol chases the losing team, trying to tag as many players as possible. The losing team must run back toward their own free zone, trying not to be tagged.

7. In case of a tie, the teams must go back into a huddle and choose a new symbol.

8. Anyone tagged must join the other team.

Countdown   For Grades 3-6

Setting: This game is best played indoors but can be played outdoors.

Materials: A blindfold for each participant.

Set-up: A small group, no larger than fifteen.

Procedure:

1. All players stand in an enclosed area so that no one will wander off.

2. Have each player wear a blindfold.

3. The trick is not only are the children blindfolded, but they cannot use verbal communication.

4. The leader whispers a number into each participant's ear (if there are ten people, the teacher randomly gives each player a number from 1-10).

5. The children must put themselves into numerical order holding hands without verbal communication. A time limit may be placed on the game so that children unable to find their spot will not become too discouraged.

Snake Pit   For Grades 1-6

Setting: This game is best for indoors but can be done outdoors.

Materials: Two rattles which can be made from cans or jars with beans or pebbles inside and two blindfolds.

Set-up: This game is best played with 8 or more participants.

Procedure:

1. Two players are chosen, one as the pursuer or "it" and one being pursued.

2. The remaining players form a circle called the pit, around the two players.

3. The two players in the middle are blindfolded and are each given a rattle.

4. The object of the game is for "it" to tag the other blindfolded player.

5. For the pursuer to locate the one being pursued, or vice-versa either one must shake their rattle, having the other immediately respond with a shake of his/or her rattle.

6. The key is that the pursuer is allowed only 5 shakes to locate the other player, while the other player can rattle as much as he or she wants to.

7. The job of the other children forming the pit is to ensure that the blindfolded players stay inside the circle. They can also help the pursuer keep count of his or her shakes.

Fruit Basket Upset   For Any Grade

Setting: Indoors

Materials: A chair for every player.

Set-up: This must be done with at least 12 children.

1. Have the children or teacher write down the name of or draw a fruit on a piece of paper, giving at least two people the same fruit.

2. Place the chairs in a circle with one chair in the middle.

3. Explain the rules of the game and stress that there is NO RUNNING!

Procedure:

1. One child is picked to be the storyteller.

2. The rest of the children sit down in a chair; there should be one chair for every participant.

3. The storyteller goes around to each child and gives them a piece of paper with the fruit on it.

4. The storyteller sits in the middle and begins to tell a story. When he or she mentions a fruit in the story such as, "and the boy ate an APPLE!", all who were assigned as apples must get up and find another vacant seat, without talking.

5. The storyteller also tries to find a seat.

6. The person left without a seat sits in the middle and becomes the storyteller.

7. If the storyteller uses the phrase "FRUIT BASKET UPSET!" in the story, then all players must get up and find a new seat.

Comments: There are many variations of this game. Any words can be substituted for fruit, such as colors, TV shows, animals, etc.

Cats and Dogs   For Grades K-5

Setting: A large space, indoors or outdoors.

Materials: Wrapped candy, prizes or other items to be hidden, two large paper or plastic bags.

Set-up:

1. This is best done with a large group – 20 children or more.

2. Adults or non-participants must hide the candy or prizes, being careful to have a variety of hiding places – some very easy to find and others more challenging.

Procedure:

1. The children are divided into teams.

2. A leader is chosen for each team and given a bag to collect candy or prizes. (If the groups are very large, two leaders can be chosen or divide into three or more groups.)

3. Each team is given an animal name such as cat or dog.

4. The leaders are the only people allowed to touch the candy.

5. All the cats must meow and point when they locate a piece of candy and the dogs must bark and point to the candy. They may not leave the candy until their leader has picked it up and put it in their bag.

6. If an adult sees a child other than the leader touch a piece of candy, the child is warned or out of the game.

7. The leader runs from child to child in their group and picks up the candy. The dog leader may not pick up candy found by a cat and vice-versa.

8. When all the candy is found, the teams form separate circles, count out their candy or prizes and divide them evenly.

Comments: This game makes sure that each child in a team receives equal amount of candy, nuts or small prizes. It is very loud when done indoors!

Message Hot Potato   For Grades K-3

Setting: Indoors

Materials: A small prize, several layers of paper, a pen and tape.

Set-up:

1. This project is best done with a group of 8-15 children.

2. Wrap a small prize in a piece of paper. Take a slightly larger piece of paper and write out a command such as "Say 6 rhyming words," or "Run around the circle 3 times," or "Spell a five letter word." Wrap and tape the paper with the command around the prize with the writing facing the inside. Continue to wrap commands around the prize until there is one command for every child participating.

Procedure:

1. Have the children sit in a circle.

2. Explain that each child can only have one turn to unwrap the hot potato and that they must pretend that it is hot!

3. Chant as a group "Hot potato, hot potato around you go, where you stop, nobody knows!"

4. The potato is passed quickly around the circle while the children chant. When the chant stops, the person left holding the potato opens the paper and follows the command. If the child cannot read the message, have an older child or an adult read it. If they have had a turn, they must pass it to someone who has not.

5. This continues until the last person opens the prize.

Comments: Records or music of any kind can be substituted for the chant.

The Detective Game   For Grades K-6

Setting: Both indoors and outdoors, together if possible.

Materials: Chalk, a magnifying glass (optional)

Set-up: This is best done with at least 20 children.

Procedure:

1. Children are divided into two teams. One team is the "detectives".

2. Each team chooses a captain.

3. The "detectives" team stays in an "off limits area" with the door closed, such as a classroom, for fifteen minutes. The captain of this team carries a magnifying glass.

4. The other team starts off outside the "off limits area" and decides together on a good place to hide. The hiding place must be large enough to fit the entire team. When a place is chosen the group moves towards it. The captain makes chalk arrows pointing in the direction the team is heading.

5. The team should do some back tracking to try to confuse the detectives. They should also cover as much ground as possible both indoors and out, remembering the time limit. The leader must leave arrows every few feet.

6. After fifteen minutes, the detectives look for the other team by following the arrows.

7. When the "detectives" capture the other team, the two teams change places. The second team uses another color of chalk or a different symbol such as wiggly arrows.

Comments: For indoors, rather than chalk to leave clues, other Hansel and Gretel type crumbs can be used such as: lego pieces, checkers, shapes cut out of colored paper, paper clips, and game pieces. For outdoors, bird seed can be substituted for the chalk.

Buried Treasure Hunt   For Grades K-6

Setting: Indoors and outdoors

Materials: Prizes, two cardboard boxes, paper, pencils.

Set-up: This works best with a large group of at least 20.

1. Purchase or make prizes for the treasure, making sure there is enough for every participant.

2. Decorate two cardboard boxes to put the treasure inside.

3. Decide where to bury each box of treasure. Each team's treasure box should be hidden in a different place.

4. Adults or older children write a set of clues for each team. Each clue should lead to the next clue. The clues must be labeled with the teams name and be numbered in sequence of usefulness. The final clue leads to the treasure.

5. Make some clues very easy and others more difficult.

Procedure:

1. Divide the children into two teams.

2. Choose a captain of each team, an older child who reads well is best.

3. Explain the game and that they must work together to find the treasure.

4. See which team finds the treasure first.

5. When the treasure has been found, each child receives a prize out of the box.

Comments: For smaller groups only one treasure box can be used.

A Spook House   For All Grades

A haunted house can be an exciting part of a celebration. Design your house with whatever you have handy, it does not have to be fancy or large. Please make sure that fearful children are allowed the option to NOT enter.

Suggestions for Haunting:

1. Create the sections of the house based on what children are planning to wear. A mad scientist, mummy, or witch work well inside the house. Dancers, French maids, punks and "cool dudes" are great tour guides through the house.

2. Engineer "rooms" by using large sheets of material, rope, pins, and curtains fastened together. Large cardboard boxes can also be walls. Paint them black. Long, thin cardboard boxes make wonderful coffins or sarcophagi, especially edged in gold spray paint.

3. Make tunnels with appliance boxes painted black. They can have odd things on the floor such as: rug bits, styrofoam chips, packing parts, ropes, balloons. Crepe paper or yarn can be hung off the ends to form an eerie texture on faces as children crawl through.

4. Yarn can be strung from curtains and tops of cardboard for a creepy feeling. Spider webs can be strung from yarn across entrances.

5. Classic spooky stuff like grapes for eyes and spaghetti for brains are a lot of fun but very frightening for some children, and messy to clean up.

6. The entrance and exit are important. Design door ways that are unique. A slide out into piles of balloons is an exciting finish.

7. Place children helpers strategically around the inside of the house. Provide them with flashlights or muted lights to highlight their faces, costumes, or actions.

8. Have things that swing down from the ceiling and get pulled back and forth across a walking area. Use a rope and a hidden child for this.

9. Music is a very important part of the effect. Use spooky, scary sounds or music. These can be bought or created by the children making the house. Have a tape that is long enough, or a child placed to aim the speakers and replay the tape.

10. Send children through the house in small groups escorted by a child with a flashlight.

11. Fluorescent paint is a wonderful decoration and fans make "spirit winds."

12. Be creative and have fun!

Appendices

Resources

NAA Keys to Quality

Reproducible Charts

Index of Activities

Resources

All of the resources listed in these pages can be found in the School-Age NOTES After-School Catalog, along with many other resources not listed here. Call 800-410-8780 to request a catalog, or go to the website at **www.AfterSchoolCatalog.com**.

General Resources on After-School Care Programming

Blakley, Barbara, et al. *Activities for School-Age Child Care*. Washington D.C.: National Association for the Education of Young Children. 2001.

Bender, Judith, Charles H. Flatter, & Jeanette M. Sorrentino. *Half A Childhood: Quality Programs for Out-of-School Time*, 3rd Ed. Nashville: School-Age NOTES. 2005.

California Department of Education. *Kids' Time: A School-Age Program Guide*. Sacramento: CDE. 1994.

Fink, Dale B. *Discipline in School-Age Care: Control the Climate, Not the Children*. Nashville: School-Age NOTES. 1995, 2004.

Koralek, Derry G., Roberta L. Newman, & Laura J. Colker. *Caring for Children in School-Age Programs*. 2 Volume Set plus Trainer's Guide. Washington D.C.: Teaching Strategies. 1995.

National Association of Elementary School Principals. *After-School Programs & the K-8 Principal*. Alexandria, VA: NAESP. 1999.

Newman, Roberta L. *Building Relationships with Parents and Families in School-Age Programs*. Nashville: School-Age NOTES.1998.

—. *Training New After-School Staff: Welcome to the World of School-Age Care!* Nashville: School-Age NOTES. 2002.

Scofield, Richard, Ed. *Summer Program Tips, Strategies & Activities for School-Agers 5-14 Years Old*. Nashville: School-Age NOTES. 2001.

Wallace, Edna. *Summer Sizzlers & Magic Mondays: School-Age Theme Activities*. Nashville: School-Age NOTES. 1994.

Whitaker, David L. *After-School Transition Activities: The Ready...Set...Go Guide to Strategies That Work*. Nashville: School-Age NOTES. 2003.

—. *Multiple Intelligences & After-School Environments: Keeping ALL Children in Mind*. Nashville: School-Age NOTES. 2002.

Resources for Middle-School Programming

Dahlstrom, Lorraine M. *Writing Down the Days: 365 Creative Journaling Ideas for Young People*. Minneapolis: Free Spirit Publishing. 2000.

Lewis, Barbara A. *The Kid's Guide to Service Projects*. Minneapolis: Free Spirit Publishing. 1995.

—. *What Do You Stand For? A Kids' Guide to Building Character*. Minneapolis: Free Spirit Publishing. 1998.

McElherne, Linda N., M.A. *Jump Starters: Quick Classroom Activities That Develop Self-Esteem, Creativity, and Cooperation*. Minneapolis: Free Spirit Publishing. 1999.

Mecca, Judy Truesdell. *Character Education Book of Plays: Middle Grade Level*. Nashville: Incentive Publications. 2001.

Newman, Roberta L. *I.D.E.A.s: Creating Successful Out-of-School Experiences in Programs for Older School-Age Children and Youth*. Cape Charles, VA: NewRoads Media. 2004.

Newman, Roberta L. et al. *Real World Connections: Theme-Based Resources and Activities for Working with 9-12 Year Olds*. Originally published by Work/Family Directions. Only available from School-Age NOTES.

Rhatigan, Joe, and Heather Smith. *Geography Fun: Cool Activities & Projects for Young Explorers*. New York: Lark Books. 2002.

Work/Family Directions. *By Design: A New Approach to Programs for 10-15 Year Olds*. 2-volume set. Nashville: School-Age NOTES. 1998.

Resources for Academic Enhancement & Support

Edwards, Sue & Kathleen Martinez. *Fun Literacy Activities for After-School Programs: Books & Beyond*. Nashville: School-Age NOTES. 2004.

Murphy, Pat, et al. *The Math Explorer: Games & Activiites for Middle School Youth Groups*. Emeryville CA: Key Curriculum Press. 2003.

National Institute on Out-of-School-Time. *Homework Assistance & Out-of-School Time/Literacy: Exploring Strategies to Enhance Learning in After-SchoolPrograms*. Nashville: School-Age NOTES. 2001.

—. *Links to Learning: A Curriculum Planning Guide for After-School Programs*. Nashville: School-Age NOTES. 2005.

Radenciich, Marguerite C., & Jeanne S. Schumm. *How to Help Your Child with Homework*. Minneapolis: Free Spirit Publishing. 1997.

Zaslavsky, Claudia. *Math Games & Activities from Around theWorld*. Chicago: Chicago Review Press. 1998.

Resources for Conflict Resolution

Divinyi, Joyce. *Good Kids, Difficult Behavior*. Atlanta: The Wellness Connection. 2002.

Kreidler, William. *Creative Conflict Resolution*.Parsippany, NJ: Good Year Books. 1984.

— and Lisa Furlong. *Advertures in Peacemaking: A Conflict Resolution Activity Guide for School-Age Programs*. Cambridge: Educators for Social Responsibility. 1995.

Lewis, Barbara A. *Being Your Best: Character Building for Kids 7-10*. Minneapolis: Free Spirit Publishing.

Ollhoff, Jim and Laurie. *Getting Along: Teaching Social Skills to Children and Youth*. Eden Prairie MN: Sparrow Media Group. 2004.

Resources for Arts & Crafts

Frank, Marjorie. *I Can Make a Rainbow!* Nashville: Incentive Publishing. 1976.

Gould, Roberta. *The Kids' Book of Incredibly Fun Crafts*. Charlotte VT: Williamson Publishing. 2003.

Kohl, MaryAnn F., and Jean Potter. *Storybook Art*. Bellingham WA: Bright Ring Publishing. 2003.

— and Kim Solga. *Discovering Great Artists*. Bellingham WA: Bright Ring Publishing. 1997.

Milord, Susan. *Adventures in Art: Arts & Crafts Experiences for 8- to 13-Year-Olds*. Charlotte VT: Williamson Publishing. 1997.

Resources for Multicultural Activities

Barbarash, Lorraine. *Multicultural Games*. Champaign IL: Human Kinetics. 1997.

Braman, Arlette N. *Kids Around the World Create!* New York: John Wiley & Sons. 1999.

Cook, Deanna F. *Kids' Multicultural Cookbook*. Charlotte VT: Williamson Publishing. 1995

Terzian, Alexandra M. *Kids' Multicultural Art Book*. Charlotte VT: Williamson Publishing. 1993.

Resources for Games

Foster, David R. and James L. Overholt. *Indoor Action Games for Elementary Children*. West Nyack NY: Parker Publishing. 1989.

Gregson, Bob, *The Incredible Indoor Games Book*. Grand Rapids: McGraw-Hill. 2004.

—. *The Outrageous Outdoor Games Book*. Grand Rapids: McGraw-Hill. 1984.

LeFevre, Dale N. *Best New Games*. Champaign IL: Human Kinetics. 2002.

Luvmour, Sambhava & Josette. *Everyone Wins!* Gabriola Island, BC: New Society Publishers.

Michaelis, Bill and John M. O'Connell. *The Game and Play Leader's Handbook.* State College PA: Venture Publishing. 2004.

Strong, Todd & Dale LeFevre. *Parachute Games.* Champaign IL: Human Kinetics. 1996.

Whitaker, David L. *Games, Games, Games: Creating Hundreds of Group Games & Sports.* Nashville: School-Age NOTES. 1996.

Resources for Science & Nature

Churchill, E. Richard, et al. *365 Simple Science Experiments with Everyday Materials.* New York: Sterling Publishing. 1997.

Frank, Marjorie. *202 Science Investigations.* Nashville: Incentive Publications. 1990.

Milord, Susan. *Kids' Nature Book.* Charlotte VT: Williamson Publishing. 1989.

Potter, Jean. *Nature in a Nutshell for Kids.* New York: John Wiley & Sons. 1995.

—. *Science in Seconds for Kids.* New York: John Wiley & Sons. 1995.

36 Keys to Quality Standards

The Standards for Quality, developed by the National AfterSchool Association (NAA), formerly known as the National School-Age Care Alliance (NSACA), include six component areas with 36 keys to define quality in programs:

Human Relationships

1. Staff relate to all children and youth in positive ways.
2. Staff responds appropriately to individual needs of children and youth.
3. Staff encourages children and youth to make choices and to become more responsible.
4. Staff interacts with children and youth to help them learn.
5. Staff uses positive techniques to guide the behavior of children and youth.
6. Children and youth generally interact with one another in positive ways.
7. Staff and families interact with each other in positive ways.
8. Staff works well together to meet the needs of children and youth.

Indoor Environment

9. The program's indoor space meets the needs of children and youth.
10. The indoor space allows children and youth to take initiative and explore their interests.

Outdoor Environment

11. The outdoor play area meets the needs of children and youth, and the equipment allows them to be independent and creative.

Activities

12. The daily schedule is flexible, and it offers enough security, independence and stimulation to meet the needs of all children and youth.
13. Children and youth can choose from a wide variety of activities.
14. Activities reflect the mission of the program and promote the development of all the children and youth in the program.

Health, Safety and Nutrition

15. There are sufficient materials to support program activities.
16. The safety and security of children and youth are protected.
17. The program provides an environment that protects and enhances the health of children and youth.
18. The program staff tries to protect and enhance the health of children and youth.

19. Children and youth are carefully supervised to maintain safety.
20. The program serves foods and drinks that meet the needs of children and youth.

Administration and Supervision

21. Staff-child ratios and group sizes permit the staff to meet the needs of children and youth.
22. Children and youth are supervised at all times.
23. Staff supports families' involvement in the program.
24. Staff, families and schools shares important information to support the well-being of children and youth.
25. The program builds links to the community.
26. The program's indoor space meets the needs of staff.
27. The outdoor space is large enough to meet the needs of children, youth and staff.
28. Staff, children and youth work together to plan and implement suitable activities, which are consistent with the program's philosophy.
29. Program policies and procedures are in place to protect the safety of the children and youth.
30. Program policies exist to protect and enhance the health of all children and youth.
31. All staff is professionally qualified to work with children and youth.
32. Staff (paid, volunteer, and substitute) are given an orientation to the job before working with children and youth.
33. The training needs of the staff are assessed, and training is relevant to the responsibilities of each job. Assistant Group Leaders receive at least 15 hours of training annually. Group Leaders receive at least 18 hours of training annually. Senior Group Leaders receive at least 21 hours of training annually. Site Directors receive at least 24 hours of training annually Program Administrators receive at least 30 hours of training annually.
34. Staff receives appropriate support to make their work experience positive.
35. The administration provides sound management of the program.
36. Program policies and procedures are responsive to the needs of children, youth and families in the community.

For more information on how to have your after-school program accredited through the **National AfterSchool Association**, go to the organization's website at **www.naaweb.org** or call 800-617-8242.

Reproducible Charts

Throughout the text are tips and suggestions on various subjects that can be useful in training after-school staff. We have reproduced these charts again in this section in order to facilitate the training aspect of a program. For training purposes only, these charts may be reproduced as handouts or for overhead projection.

The charts included in this section include:

8 Suggestions to Communicate Effectively with Parents

9 Tips for Guiding Children's Behavior

8 Tips for Effective Shared Space

6 Suggestions for a Successful Group Time

7 Hints for a Successful Rest Time

10 Hints for a Successful Program for Older Children

Middle-School Program Tips

9 Strategies for Planning a Summer Camp Program

Summer Theme Ideas/Ideas for Special Events

11 Hints for Successful Field Trips

8 suggestions to communicate effectively with parents

1. Learn parents' names and try to greet them every time they enter the program.

2. Ask families to share information about their lifestyle – the intake or enrollment form is a good place to gather this type of information. Remember to be sensitive to and respectful of their privacy.

3. Say something positive about their child whenever possible. Creating a positive relationship first can make more difficult conversations easier later on.

4. Respect parental confidences.

5. Discuss only essential details of incidents and avoid naming other children involved whenever possible.

6. Timing is important; it takes practice and patience to learn that some things can wait.

7. In your newsletter or handbook include a section about going home and transition times. Offer suggestions and resources on issues or concerns families are facing.

8. Remember, a sense of humor is essential when working with parents and their children.

9 Tips for Guiding Children's Behavior

- Staff must understand that behavior has meaning. Staff should observe for patterns in children and youth behavior that can help identify possible causes when problems occur and find effective ways to deal with the problems.

- Staff must use observation as a means to understand a child's behavior. The observations of the entire staff can help understand a child's behavior and actions and help define a course of action.

- Staff must know the children and youth enrolled in the program, be familiar with family history, the child or youth's experience during their academic day and how the child or youth interacts socially with peers and staff.

- Staff needs to create an environment that is safe, consistent and provides continuity. Many times, a child's challenging behaviors can be addressed through the environment. Schedule, room arrangement, activities offered, snack, interactions with peers and adults and children's health or well being can affect behavior.

- School-age staff must be aware that each child or youth is an individual with unique needs, abilities and interests.

- Staff need to be skilled in problem-solving techniques and understand that the "one shoe fits all" solution does not always work. There are strategies staff can learn about problem solving, individualizing and creating continuity and consistency. Staff should carefully determine who owns the problem and who or what is causing the problem.

- Staff must understand their job is to guide rather than manage so that the child or youth can learn the skills necessary for life beyond the program. Staff should help a child or youth learn to make good choices about their behavior and to assist them in identifying the problem, generating options for resolving the problem and choosing ways to help each child get his or her needs met. When a child makes a poor choice, staff use the opportunity as a means to help the child discover new options and ways to handle the same problem better.

- Staff should be familiar with and utilize several behavior guidance techniques. Staff should work to build skills, build self-esteem and confidence and help to develop life-skill strategies for dealing with conflict, choice making and day-to-day living.

- Staff should have resources available to help deal with behaviors that are far more challenging than everyday-type behaviors. These resources should include training, mental health consultation, community resources, books and each other.

8 tips for effective shared space

1. Interest areas can still be set up on a daily basis. To define areas use tables or shelves with wheels, bulletin boards or folding storage cabinets.

2. Large pillows, bean bag chairs, pop-up tents, small folding camp chairs and small area rugs can substitute for heavier quiet-area furniture.

3. Portable signs, bulletin boards on wheels and backs of shelves can be used to define and label the learning centers and serve as room dividers.

4. Pegboard is an excellent versatile material for hanging things, making room dividers, and enclosing areas for privacy.

5. Art supplies can be stored on wheeled shelves – use containers such as baskets, large cans and tins, covered ice cream tubs or chicken buckets, and shoe boxes.

6. Removable carpet squares can be used for the quiet and group sections because they are easily stacked.

7. Plastic stackable containers on wheels work for movable cubbies.

8. The use of "spill-over space," such as a hall and special rooms, is great for doing small-group projects.

6 suggestions for a successful group time

1. Vary the length, depending on the age and attention span of the children. Younger children need a shorter time. Vary the group size. Try to make your groups as small as possible so that all children can participate, listen and be heard by the staff and the group.

2. Begin group time with an activity to grab their attention and interest. Use activities that build and develop the team or group. Engage their senses. Then the group will be more able to listen or participate.

3. Pace your activities by watching the children's reactions. It is easy to tell when they are bored or restless. Change your tempo accordingly. Do not hesitate to throw out an activity that is not working. Spontaneous activities are perfectly valid.

4. Separate children who have trouble sitting next to each other before starting group time. Another way is to have an adult keep a sharp lookout for trouble. By having adults sit down with the children unobtrusively and in strategic locations many difficulties can be avoided, making it more enjoyable for everyone.

5. Allow a disruptive child to sit or draw at a nearby table rather than letting the disruption continue.

6. Do not limit group time to the indoors or the school grounds. Children need time outside each day and like to experience new places or visit old favorite ones.

7 hints for a successful rest time

1. Before rest time, have a group time to calm the children down and have them use the bathroom.

2. Always have the children use the same cot or mat labeled with their name on it. Have each child bring a sheet, blanket and pillow from home, including whatever small item helps them to be more comfortable. Cots and linens should be cleaned weekly.

3. Allow children to take books to their cots. After five minutes or so, have all books put under cots and turn out the lights.

4. Limit napping to one hour; longer periods tend to result in children having trouble falling asleep at bedtime.

5. Make a chart of who sleeps and who does not the first week of school; arrange the children around the room accordingly. Strategically place the non-sleepers in places where they do not disturb the sleepers. After a half-hour of resting, quiet alternative activities can be made available for non-sleepers.

6. Always place the child's cot or mat in the same place in the room.

7. Rub the backs of children to help them fall asleep; it can work wonders! Many children who never take naps will often fall asleep if their backs are rubbed. Back rubbing can be combined with verbal and physical reinforcement for those who are resting quietly. It really does calm down those who are fidgety and allows their bodies to relax. However, some children do not like their backs rubbed and the caregiver must respect the child's wishes. Some programs also have quiet music, adults singing, or taped stories during rest time.

10 hints for a successful program for older children

1. Provide a space or area just for them. Separate rooms are the best solution. If this is not possible, try setting up a corner of the room for them. Make this area off-limits for any younger child. Include in this area: age-appropriate games, a rug, a sofa, and bean-bag chairs or futons, a tape recorder/radio, art supplies, models, etc. In addition, equipment such as a Caroom™ board, ping-pong table, air hockey and a pool table are appropriate. Nerf™ pool or ping-pong sets are great.

2. Many older children have had years of painting and process-oriented art projects. Older children are not as process oriented as younger ones and are ready for kits, models and other challenging projects. They are interested in activities that have a goal and are ready to learn techniques and work on long-term projects. They also enjoy the occasional hands-on messy project.

3. Invite the older children to be helpers for the younger children. They can assist during homework time, art time, group or snack time. The older children may want to "adopt" a younger child and be their special helper. This has been very successful in our program.

4. Allow space away from adults for the older children. Supervise them, but try to keep a proper distance; do not intrude on their personal conversations and space unless it is necessary for safety.

5. Social problem solving and group dynamics are very important for the older group of children. Teachers need to help build a sense of group acceptance and togetherness.

6. Older children must learn to take responsibility for themselves and their actions. They can help establish their own rules and consequences.

7. Older children especially need ample time to exercise and be outside.

8. Outdoor games should be of their own choosing. Much socializing and modeling goes on at these times. Rules are an important part of the process. Adults should interfere only if rules are unfair or exclude some children.

9. Older children often invent their own games and play them for long periods. Encourage this process; it is important for their growth and development.

10. Older children should have a stronger voice in the program planning and implementation.

Middle-School Program Tips

- Call the program something inventive and creative, attractive to middle-school youth.

- Staff must be trained in youth development needs.

- Staff must be considered good role models.

- Middle-school youth need a separate space from the younger children.

- Middle-school youth need to have a high degree of involvement in program planning.

- Enrollment must be flexible to accommodate growing independence and other out-of-school-time activities.

- Staff must keep in mind the nutritional needs of adolescents.

- Homework assistance must be a central component of the program, as academic levels increase. Staff must be competent to help with the academic needs.

- Recreational activities and a variety of choices should be included when time permits.

- Allowing time to socialize is essential.

- Foster team-building skills.

- Service learning projects allow the youth to give back to and support the community.

- If possible, offer Friday Night Outings (FNO) or a Friday Night In (FNI) program.

9 strategies for planning a summer camp program for middle-school youth

1. Speak to the youth and ask them what activities are interesting. Include youth when planning camp, as youth "buy-in" will make a successful camp.

2. Develop a flexible program for youth. For youth attending academic summer school, provide a before-and-after-summer school program. Camp sessions should be one or two weeks in length because youth want to choose a variety of activities in the summer.

3. Provide as many opportunities as your budget and transportation system can support. Use the camp location as a home base and then use what is available in your community to help the youth explore the world around them. Field trips to amusement parks, water parks, overnight camping trips, professional sports games, laser tag, video arcades, museums, recreational areas, beaches, pools and local colleges are popular.

4. Encourage physical activity. Help youth explore a variety of physical games and sports. Sports outings such as rowing on a lake, indoor rock climbing, ice-skating, roller-skating, skateboarding, bike riding, fencing, and a visit to a pool hall can be built into the program on a weekly basis along with field trips and local outings.

5. Teach life skills. Use a counselor-in-training model for interested youth. [*At RAMS, youth volunteer as counselors-in-training, spending three hours per week working with younger children. They are supervised, receive training and have an opportunity to ask questions and problem solve about their experience working with children. They sign a contract, work with center staff and are evaluated.*]

6. Allow the youth to create businesses to raise money. The money can be used to offset the cost of field trips that are more expensive or as a donation to an organization of the youth's choice. Youth are responsible for the planning, implementing and evaluating of the endeavor. This is a good opportunity to learn about setting and achieving goals, accounting and retailing, and social skills.

7. Specialty camps are great for this group. Camps that focus on science, sports, visual or performing arts, computers, outdoor skills or music are big draws. If you plan to offer a specialty camp, keep room in your schedule for some traditional camp activities to balance the camp experience.

8. Involve the families. Offer family nights for youth to highlight what they are doing or have learned in camp. Family night can be a potluck dinner or youth can serve dinner to their family. You can even make it a fundraiser.

9. Youth and their families should evaluate the camp each summer. Use their comments to improve the program for the next summer.

Summary Theme Ideas:

Ecology	Animals	Under the Sea	Bays
Olympics	Space and Stars	Hooray for Hollywood	Jungles
Into the Past	Toys	Sports	Myth and Fantasy
Deserts	Endangered Species	International Foods	Fads
Pets	Collections	Weather	Geography
Dinosaurs	Super Heroes	Prehistoric Times	The Gold Rush
Disneyland ™	Reptiles	Nature	Aeronautics
History	Magic	Electronics	Water Sports
Safari	Mad Scientist	Environmental Studies	Explorers
Gizmos and Gadgets	Make a Movie	World Travel	Fashion
Communication	The Seashore	Around the World	Back to the Future
Inventions	Archaeology	Let's Put On A Show	Color

Ideas for special events:

Carnival	Un-birthday Party	Lost Treasure Day	Sand Castle Contest
Puppet Show	Restaurant Day	Kite/airplane contest	Backwards Day
Winter in the Summer	Olympics	Relay Races	Office Day
Outer Space Day	Mystery Day	Square Dancing	Build a Volcano
Soap Bubble Contest	Cartoon Dress-up Day	Line Dancing	Water Mania
Sock Hop	Chinese Cooking	Mexican Cooking	Car Wash
Pet Wash	Crafts Sale	BBQ	Old Fashioned Picnic
Teddy Bear Picnic	Trading Cards Day	Lip syncing contest	Luau
Wild West Day	Crazy Hair Day	PJ Party	Secret Pals
Scavenger Hunt	Talent Show	Detective Day	
Crafts Day	Cook-Off	Mad Scientist Inventions	

11 hints for successful field trips

1. When selecting a field trip have a staff member visit the site in advance.

2. Make reservations for the field trip in advance and pay fees.

3. It is a good idea to call the place the day before to reconfirm.

4. Be well staffed; include parent volunteers if possible.

5. Each teacher of a group of children should bring along a small first-aid kit, emergency releases, tissues and/or wet wipes.

6. Dress the children in a school T-shirt (in bright colors easy to see in a crowd), or other identifying article of clothing such as a scarf or a baseball cap. Each child should bring a jacket or sweater. (*In our program, the children wear tie-dyed shirts and carry camp backpacks.*)

7. Have children bring lunches in paper bags stowed inside their backpacks (no glass containers).

8. Make sure the children know the field trip rules ahead of time, are aware of where and why they are going, and what mode of transportation is being used. Also, make sure they know what to do if they get lost from the group.

9. When walking in small groups (4-10), the adult should walk in the middle of the group (if there is only one adult). For larger groups or situations where there are two or more adults, have one adult lead the group, one adult in the middle and one adult at the end of the line.

10. Children should never cross the street alone and should stay within the crosswalks. For crowded intersections, have one adult stand in the middle of the street to stop traffic if necessary.

11. Encourage the children to write thank you notes when appropriate.

Index of Activities